THE
VIBRANT CHURCH

A PEOPLE-BUILDING PLAN
FOR CONGREGATIONAL HEALTH

E. STANLEY OTT

GL
Regal Books
A Division of GL Publications
Ventura, California, U.S.A.

Published by Regal Books
A Division of GL Publications
Ventura, California 93006
Printed in U.S.A.

Library of Congress Cataloging-in-Publication Data

Ott, E. Stanley, 1948-
    The vibrant church.

    Bibliography: p.
    1. Church group work. 2. Church renewal. 3. Church growth. I. Title.
BV652.2.077   1989   253   89-8405
ISBN 0-8307-1261-5

1 2 3 4 5 6 7 8 9 10 / 91 90 89

To Ann Marie, Lee, Lindsay, and Shelley
God's Gifts
My Joys

Contents

Acknowledgments

I praise God for my wife, Ann Marie, who has shared over a decade of discussion about this book with me. I am grateful to Carol Lacy for her superb editorial support. Jim Tozer, my brother, fellow worker, and fellow soldier is a partner in ministry who has made a permanent difference in my life. Along with Jim Tozer, Hoyt Byrum, Tom Saxon, Lydia Sarandan, Joe Ely, Dick Feiertag, Anella McFee, Marsha Lowe, Matt Boyers, and Steve Resch, Jr., I have been privileged to serve in ministry with the vibrant people of Covenant Presbyterian Church. I deeply appreciate the friendship and leadership of Chuck Miller. It was he who introduced me to the concept of a biblical process of ministry.

I am grateful to many who helped with this project: Dave Dilling, Neal Fearnot, Ed Hargitt, and Mike McIntire; to Heidi Smith, Julie Hultman Chalmers, Jan Cooper, Shura McKinney, and Thelma Bishop who typed years of preliminary drafts; to Dottie White for her effort in producing the final copy; and to many partners in ministry including Bob Chalmers, Lewis and Carol Christiansen, Bill Dalton, Tom Schwartz, Dan Draney, Dave and Shirley Eads, Neal and Sharon Fearnot, John Stewart, Steve Ebling, Dave Eikenberry, John Walker, Bob and Terry Tucker, Jill Reynolds, Bill Ruwe, and Bob Grosso.

E. Stanley Ott

Introduction:
People or Program?

Boy! Sometimes I get so discouraged." Janet plopped down in a chair in the pastor's office. "I seem to spend so much time and effort trying to get a good program going that will minister to women. Just about the time it looks as if it's going to take off, a key person quits, or attendance drops, or some other activity takes my best workers away. What am I doing wrong?"

Do you ever feel like this? One summer I was struggling with similar questions while I attended a three-week session at a Chicago seminary. Away from my duties at church and my responsibilities at home, I was able to think about my life. I was asking basic questions like: What are we doing in our church about ministry? What is the purpose of "program"? What is ministry?

I was also starting to question my own career future. I had been responsible for running eight program areas at Covenant Presbyterian Church in Lafayette, Indiana. A heavy task. The church had called Hoyt Byrum, a friend of mine, to join the staff and take over three of those programs as part of his responsibilities. That was great news. I was thrilled that Hoyt was coming. But this caused me to question my own ministry effectiveness and my future. Am I going to spend the next 40 years running five programs? If someone comes up to me when I am ready to retire and asks me, "Well, Stan, what did you do with your life?" will I have to answer, "I ran five programs," or "I had a large college group and a great evangelism ministry, and I attended more than 400 couples' fellowship meetings!"

Is this what Jesus meant when He said to "go and make disciples"? I did not think so. As I struggled and prayed over this concern, God guided me to realize that my focus was wrong. Even though all of these programs involved many people, and even though they were good in themselves, I realized that I was not making disciples, I was making programs. What I had to do was find out how the Bible describes a maturing Christian and how I could go about building that person.

That is what this book is about—how you can build a vibrant church that makes Christian disciples who don't just bask in program, but who share in ministry. In it we describe four patterns for building people, any of which you can adapt for your church. (See fig. 1.) Each of the four sections in the book is geared to help you grasp the essential ingredients of a people-building ministry and to apply them in your church or ministry opportunities.

Section I addresses the ingredients of ministry—

People, Principles, and Practice—and discusses the significance of the individual and corporate aspects of the church for ministry.

In Section II we look at how you may combine the ingredients of ministry in the first of four basic patterns for building people in your congregation: Person-to-person ministry.

Section III—With "The Ends and Means of Ministry to the Group," we address the corporate aspect of the Body of Christ, or how to build the *fellowship* in the image of Christ.

Then in Section IV we get down to business with the "The Practice of People-Building Ministry"—the Small Group, the Small Group Movement, and the Discipleship Community.

As you gain an overview of the three ingredients of ministry and how to use them, you can begin to assess the unique needs of the people with whom you are in ministry. You will be able to review the basic principles of ministry that are essential to building people in well-being and Christian discipleship. You will be ready to adapt one of the four basic people-building patterns into a program for your church and into your own personal ministry. See Appendix H for a checklist of all the people-building guides.

Patterns for Building People

Pattern 1: Person to Person Ministry

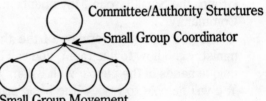

Pattern 2: The Small Group

Small Group Leader

Small Group

Pattern 3: The Small Group Movement
Within the Congregation

Committee/Authority Structures

Small Group Coordinator

Small Group Movement

Pattern 4: The Discipleship Community
Within the Congregation

Committee/Authority Structures

Community Leader

Ministry Team

Small Group Coordinator

Discipleship Community

Figure 1

SECTION I
A BLUEPRINT FOR AN EQUIPPING MINISTRY

CHAPTER 1

A Vibrant Church

A warm, vibrant, exciting congregation is the dream of every pastor, church leaders and church member. But just what *is* a vibrant church? A wealth of programs? A large attendance in worship? A big staff? If that's all there is, then 90 percent of all churches are not now vibrant and never will be! Of course, programs, staff, and worship attendance may indicate a vibrant church, but there is something more basic.

To be vibrant is to pulse with life and energy. A vibrant church may be large or small, but it has a vibrant Lord—Jesus Christ, literally alive and present, and a vibrant people—individuals engaged in Christian discipleship, growing in Christ and enabling others to grow in Christ.

A church may have few programs and no staff and yet be vibrant. *Every* church can be a vibrant church!

There are two approaches to building a vibrant church:

The church can begin with renewing and discipling the individual; or, the church can first define its purpose and then revitalize its organization or structure around some well-defined goals. Both approaches are essential; to do one without the other, ultimately leads to the end of renewal.

In most situations, the place to start is with personal renewal. Personal renewal happens when we winsomely offer the *message* of new life in Christ and the *ministry* that builds active disciples. We pray for renewal, knowing it is always the result of God's work among the people.

Revitalizing the church through defining goals and reorganizing can be very satisfying for leaders and people alike. There is the sense that "we are getting somewhere." But caution: Organization merely creates the framework within which life grows—the skeleton on which life hangs. Structure is essential to life, but structure is not all there is to life. Even if you reorganized the parts of a lifeless body, it would still be lifeless! That is why I suggest that you begin renewal in your church through the first approach—renewing and discipling people. Ultimately, both discipleship ministry and organizational planning must partner if renewal, once begun, is to continue.

After his first semester in seminary, a friend of mine wrote, "Stan, we have been looking for a new church home every Sunday, but they are all DOA!" Dead On Arrival! My friend found institution, he found ritual, he found empty tradition. He did not find life.

A vibrant church offers life to its people so that they:

• learn and respond to the knowledge of God

- grow in faith in Jesus Christ and in the power of the Holy Spirit
- spend daily time in Bible study and prayer
- apply Scripture to their personal lives
- develop stronger families
- feel a sense of belonging to the fellowships
- grow in deep personal friendship
- discover their gifts and use them
- grow in financial generosity
- see themselves as "sent" to serve
- offer compassion in Christ's name
- have their needs met
- share willingly their faith in Jesus Christ
- develop a world vision and a concern for mission
- grow in the life and joy of the Christian faith.

Such a church ministers to equip its people "in every good thing to do His will, working in us that which is pleasing in His sight" (Heb. 13:21), and displays a church spirit that is positive and uplifting.

The Church—A Grocery Store or a Farm?

Today's pastor typically carries three basic responsibilities: preaching, programming, pastoral care. These all receive major emphasis in seminary. People in the congregation, because of conditioning, continually reinforce their significance either by congratulating a job well done or complaining about a job undone. Under the umbrella of each kind of work is a number of major time-consuming tasks.

After a seminar in which I had taught four patterns for building discipleship in the church, I followed up on a number of pastors attendees to see how they were applying the concepts they were taught. One pastor returned home and preached seven funerals in two months. Another returned to organize a centennial anniversary celebration. Another began a building program. Another faced problems from a yoked parish. All said they were too busy to build a few people in Christ or to reorganize their program to build people more effectively.

When will these pressures of busyness end? Never! Is it any wonder that building people is often neglected? Seminaries do not teach it as a discipline and people do not generally realize that they need it, so they do not ask for it. *We fail to make it a real priority.* We assume that Sunday morning worship and other regular programs will help make disciples. Yes, programs can and do have a building effect on our spiritual lives. However, they can be much *more* effective if we consciously focus on the goal of building people rather than maintaining the program.

The difference between a church that builds people and one that merely maintains the program is like the difference between a grocery store and a farm. In a grocery store the produce arrives and is arranged and rearranged for display. Cut off from its roots, its growth is over. On a farm we see sowing, nurturing, weeding and harvesting. The farmer seeks to enable life to grow. He wants to see healthy mature fruit develop.

A ministry that emphasizes program without considering its effectiveness in building discipleship is like the grocery store. A new person arrives at the church where he is shuffled from program to program for years, like produce rearranged for display. The farmer-ministry wants to see people grow toward spiritual maturity, to see them move from wherever they are toward the image of Jesus Christ.

Without an authentic person-centered ministry, the

church, as the community of faith, will never significantly grow in faith or numbers (see Acts 16:5).

The Pastor—A Role-Player or a Goal-Maker?

Much of what is going on in Christian ministry today, both in the organized church and in parachurch groups, is outstanding and effective in its impact. However, many of us doing ministry—whether we are pastors, church members or parachurch workers—have limited views of ministry that hamper us in effectively building people.

One limited view is the *ministry of Word and sacrament in worship*: prepare and deliver the sermon and celebrate baptism and the Lord's Supper. These are essential marks of Christian life which Christ commanded us to fulfill. They honor God and minister to people. However, some people tend to concentrate their ministry on the sermon and worship leadership of the whole church as the community of faith without considering the spiritual needs of each individual. A pastor whose life centers on Word, sacrament, and pastoral care can easily see himself as the only real shepherd of the flock; thereby stifling the dynamics of shared ministry. Pastors are shepherds whose ministry is both to tend the sheep in their care and also to train and send those sheep to shepherd others.

A second limited view, nearly the opposite of the first one, occurs when much disciple building is *focused on the individual*, but little is centered on developing the whole fellowship or church or on the significance of the sacraments. This frequently occurs in parachurch groups and in ministry to people outside the institutional church.

A third limited view of ministry is *"pastoral care."* Pastoral care once meant ministry to the whole person— physically and spiritually, and in some quarters still does.

However, much of the focus of contemporary pastoral care is on encouragement, healing, and presence in times of need rather than on spiritual growth. A parent cares for a sick child in order to see the child healed. The ultimate goal of every good parent, however, is to encourage and enable that child into mature adulthood. Caring ministry that builds well-being is essential to the process of building people, but it is only one aspect of the total ministry to the Body of Christ.

Another partial view of ministry is a *program mentality*. This view is concerned only with administering worship services, Sunday Schools, visitation programs, evangelism, men's and women's groups and other programs. If this is your primary view of ministry, you will frequently find yourself totally concerned with arranging program details: who will teach, who will bring the refreshments, what publicity is needed. This view of ministry can easily produce programs for "people without faces," and the individual is lost in the details of planning and administering.

We generally tend to evaluate success by the size, pizazz, and publicity of a given program or congregational event, such as a church renewal week, vacation Bible school, music program, or seminar. This emphasis tends to give the impression that if you are "really in ministry," you must have committee responsibility and lead a program whether you are a pastor or a member of the church. Programs are essential to ministry, yet they are only one facet of a total view of ministry.

A final limited view of ministry is *that which an ordained minister does*. As an ordained minister I love to minister, but *all* Christians are called to do ministry. "And He gave some as . . . pastors and teachers, for the equipping of the *saints* [Christians] for the *work of service [ministry]*, to the building up of the body of Christ" (Eph. 4:11-

12, italics added). Pastors and teachers are the "equippers" of every Christian, offering the training needed so that he and she may minister to and build up the Body of Christ. Ministry is, in fact, to be a shared ministry—shared by pastors and people.

Of course, all of these practices are essential to a total ministry. We need to teach the Word, minister the sacraments, build the individual, provide pastoral care and organize programs. When they are all done well, together they become a tremendous source of life and strength to the church or fellowship. However, applying and administering all of these facets is more than the pastor can handle alone. Expecting your church to offer all of these traditional views of ministry has two major consequences.

First, pastors often build their entire lives around the traditional views of ministry and become absorbed in the roles of preaching, programs, and pastoral care. The focus in such cases is on the *roles* of ministry rather than the *goals* of ministry. A traditional role-oriented pastor easily becomes swallowed up in maintenance, working to keep people's involvement and activity level high, and offering help in time of need. This concept extends to the congregation as well. Church members model these roles, often seeing themselves as teachers, committee members or caregivers with no self-concept that says, "I am sent to build another person in Christ." Of course, each of these roles, properly practiced, does have a nurturing impact on the Body of Christ, but they tend to become ends of ministry rather than the means of ministry.

Second, people tend to let the pastor do the work of the ministry—and the pastor often wants to do it alone. As one man said to the pastor at a church dinner, "You pray, that's what we pay you for!" Scripture, however, calls us to equip members of the Body for ministry.

The Ministry—The Pastor's or the People's?

The term "ministry" comes from the Greek word *diaconia*, and our Bibles often translate *diaconos* as "minister" or "deacon." It means "servant." Ministry is service. The *model* of ministry is Jesus: "For even the Son of Man did not come to be served, but to serve, and to give His life a ransom for many" (Mark 10:45).

The goal of servant ministry is clear in Paul's letter to the Ephesians: "And He gave some as apostles, and some as prophets, and some as evangelists, and some as pastors and teachers, for the equipping of the saints for the work of service [*diaconia—ministry*], to the building up of the body of Christ; until we all attain to the unity of the faith, and of the knowledge of the Son of God, to a mature man, to the measure of the stature which belongs to the fullness of Christ" (4:11-13).

Note that the primary task of the pastor and teacher is not the work of the ministry, per se, but the "equipping of the saints" to do the work of the ministry. An equipping ministry aims at preparing you, making you competent in your ministry to others. In order to build you in Christ, I would care for you, disciple you, and equip you to do the same for others. Even though most churches have majored in caring ministries and offer excellent Christian education opportunities, they have not been very effective in equipping their people to personally minister to others.

When a person or congregation learns to build people in Christ and to equip others to do the same, then God, by grace, builds the vibrant church.

One morning, sitting in a long meeting, I noticed a friend sitting nearby, busily drawing diagrams of football plays. Little Xs and Os going this way and that. Seeing it reminded me of the old story about the coach who excitedly diagramed his new football play on the blackboard with Xs and Os, defense and offense going this way and that. Finally, he turned to the team and asked, "What do you think men?"

A fellow in the back put up his hand and said, "Coach, I think that's a fantastic play. I have just one question."

"What is it Smith?"

"Coach, are we Xs or are we Os?"

I love that story! As I watched my friend drawing his diagrams, I began to think, "You know, I'm an X. I'm a defensive player. I need other people to take the initiative in my life, others to build my faith, to build my life in Christ, to encourage my heart."

But then it occurred to me, "I'm also an O. I'm on the offense. I am to take the initiative and go to you, build your faith, meet your needs, minister to your situation." I am both X and O — receiver and giver, learner and teacher, sheep and shepherd. You too are both X and O; you too are receiver and giver at the same time. So, when we treat people in the church only as receivers, as sheep ("Come attend our program and be fed, or see our pastor if you have a problem"), we only perform half a ministry We must both tend one another *and* send one another. We must seek to build people in Christ and to equip them to build others in Christ.

In truth, we *are* all sheep. We will always be sheep. As Jesus said, "My sheep hear My voice, and I know them, and they follow Me" (John 10:27). At the same time, however, He is calling every one of us to become shepherds. As we grow in the image of Christ and become like Him, then, like Jesus, we will grow a heart for people, a desire to build others in Christ. Churches must challenge people to develop a heart for people. Leaders must equip them to serve one another, and then must model the dual role of a sheep needing care and a shepherd offering care.

One of the dilemmas of the current traditional role of pastor (which literally means shepherd), is that a congregation tends to see itself as a flock having the pastor as the only shepherd, or else the pastoral staff plus the ruling elders and deacons as the shepherds. The expectation is that those leader-type people will do all the shepherding and carry out the functions of teaching, leading and pastoral care, leaving the rest of us free to participate as we choose.

The majority of American Christians are passive in ministry. Only a fraction of the total membership of most churches occupy positions of leadership. When the circle of people who are equipped and committed to building a vibrant church widens to include more and more people in addition to the church's leaders, tremendous power is released within the church by the grace of God.

You may or may not consider yourself a leader, but lead you must if God is to work through your service to build His people into a vibrant church. We often speak of people who are in "positions of leadership." We think of presidents, managers, principals, pastors, elders, and deacons as leaders by virtue of their office. However, leadership is not a position but a practice. It is not an office you hold, although your office may provide an opportunity for you to lead, but leadership is something you do. It is a practice.

There are three elements in leadership. First, a leader knows where he or she is going—a *purpose*. Second, a leader has a way to get where he or she is going—a *plan*. Finally, a leader has others going along with him or her—a *people*. A person who does not have all three elements is not a leader.

A *leader with a purpose* knows where he is going and

what has to be done. "Where you are going" may be the job you have to perform or it may be a goal you wish to reach. It may be a problem to be solved, something you want to teach, or an attitude you want to impart to someone else. As a leader you have to figure out where you are going based on the needs of the person to whom you minister.

Leaders, who are usually the most pressured of people, must take time to think and pray, "Lord, for my congregation [or my fellowship or my family or my work], what is the next step? Where do you want us to go?" The moment that you yield to the pressures in life and fail to take the time to discover where you and your people should be going, is when those pressures become the leader and direct your steps. Many people surrender their leadership to the busyness of their lives.

A leader has a plan. As a leader you have to solve the problems that stand in the way of getting the group where it is going. You find a way to get where you want to go. God has given the Christian leader at least three significant aids to discovering the way or the means of ministry. The first way for a Christian is a Person: "I am the way, the truth and the life." Jesus Christ is literally the Way. Trust Jesus Christ to help you develop plans for your group.

Second, not only do we have the person of Christ as the Way but we have the Word of Christ, the Scriptures, to show us the way. Of course, the Bible does not lay out specific answers for all the particular challenges of ministry you may face; however, the Scriptures *do* give wisdom and principles of ministry you need if you are to find the way.

Third, you have access to wise people to help you to

discover the way the to develop the plans. "Without consultation, plans are frustrated, but with many counselors they succeed" (Prov. 15:22). A wise leader includes his or her people in the process of discovering the way and developing plans as one means of winning their participation. *A shared ministry requires a shared leadership.*

This matter of finding the way and developing a plan is one of the most difficult tasks of leadership. Often you will know what needs must be met, what problems solved, what has to be done; but knowing *how* to follow through can be difficult. It is the mature leader who trusts God, searches the Scriptures, and seeks wise counsel in selecting the best plan for his or her group. Failure to plan is another way many people surrender their leadership.

Finally, a leader has people following. Even though you have a *purpose*, and a *plan* for how to get there, you cannot lead without a following. A leader is a person who sees what has to be done and gets it done *with* others. You can know where you should go with your people, your family, your church, your work, and you can plan the way to get there, but practicing the plan and keeping people with you demands personal courage, tact and sensitivity, and moment-by-moment faith in the power of the Holy Spirit. If you know where you are going and how to get there, but lack the courage to ask people to be with you, then you simply surrender your leadership to your fears!

CHAPTER 2

The Double Focus of Ministry

D o you know what held the bricks together in the Tower of Babel? Bituminous tar. The builders baked uneven bricks and used tar to join them together. I wonder, if God had not intervened, how long the tar would have lasted in the hot sun of Shinar and under such a heavy load.

Do you know what the Hebrews used to hold together the stones of the great Temple?

Surprisingly, they used nothing! The stones were cut to fit each other exactly. Their rough edges were removed and their sides cut to fit together. Some of the stones were very small, and others were huge, weighing several tons apiece.

To build the great Temple, the Hebrew architect had to exercise a double focus in building. He had to keep one eye on each stone to ensure that it would properly fit with its neighbors, and he had to keep the other eye on the entire Temple to make sure each side was straight, each column vertical, and each floor level.

Those of us in ministry—both pastors and church members—also have to exercise a double focus in building the church. The meaning of the double focus in ministry came to me one year when my wife, Ann Marie, and I were sent by our church to a leadership conference. A number of programs were offered as models for ministry. As I sat there in the workshop I thought, *Well, Lord, we're already doing many of these programs at Covenant and we're doing them well. Why all the emphasis on program?* Instantly the thought came: God gathers His people into a group—a body—a portion of the Body of Christ, the visible Church. This body is also supposed to mature in Christ. Program is simply one of our methods of enabling the group to grow to health and maturity.

Now I had something else to wonder about. What is a "mature" group? For years I had been thinking about what a mature Christian *person* is, but a mature Christian *group* involved many things about which I was completely ignorant. If there are *two* aspects of the Body of Christ—the person and the group—then it will take a double focus of ministry to bring the local church and its people into the maturity the Bible speaks about.

The Temple of the Living God

Both Paul and Peter used the Temple as an example of the Body of Christ. Paul said: "Christ Jesus Himself being the

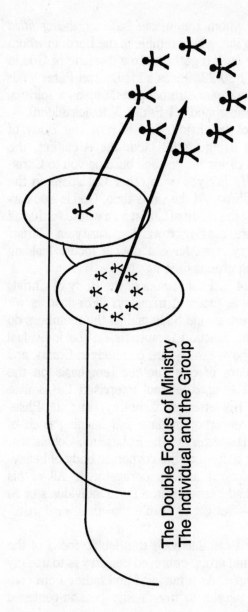

The Double Focus of Ministry
The Individual and the Group

Figure 1

corner stone, in whom the whole building, *being fitted together* is growing into a holy temple in the Lord; in whom you also *are being built* together into a dwelling of God in the Spirit" (Eph. 2:20-22, italics added). And Peter said: "You also, as *living stones*, are being built up as a spiritual house for a holy priesthood" (1 Pet. 2:5, italics added).

The Temple of the living God is now the Body of Christ. *You* are a living stone! God, the Architect, the Master Builder, is caring for you and building you to Christian maturity as He fits you with other Christians in the growing Body of Christ. At the same time, God is also caring for and building the Body of Christ as a whole so that all of us together are moving toward maturity in Christ. Therefore, ministry must have a double focus: building people and building groups (see fig. 1).

In Romans 12:4-5, Paul speaks of the Body of Christ, clarifying the double focus of ministry: "For just as we have many members in one body and all the members do not have the same function [emphasis on the individual aspect], so we, who are many, are one body in Christ, and individually members of one another [emphasis on the group aspect]." The apostle Paul exercised the double focus of ministry. His letters to Timothy, Titus and Philemon are person-centered, guiding and building each of these three men. His letters to the Ephesians, Colossians, and Romans were written to the corporate body of believers, giving instructions and encouragement. All of his letters—whether addressed primarily to individuals or to corporate groups—sought to enable growth toward maturity.

The best way I can illustrate the double focus of the person-centered and group-centered ministry is to use my family as an example. As a husband and father I am concerned for each person in my family: person-centered ministry. Is my wife growing as a person or is she frustrated, feeling as if she were stagnating? Is each of my children receiving the proper mental, physical, emotional, social and spiritual challenges he or she needs at this point in life? And, at the same time, is my whole family interacting with one another, having fun together, being stretched in our faith together, serving one another—group-centered ministry. Are we offering ministry to others and reaching out as a family?

Maybe one of my children needs to be disciplined in some aspect of behavior and my wife needs to be hugged. How inappropriate it would be for me to discipline my whole family because of the one child when one member needs to be hugged and another member has a different need. This is person-centered ministry. Then by reading a Psalm to the whole family at the breakfast table I can help us grow together as a family in our faith in Christ.

We do not build a person or a group by isolating one aspect from the other. "The eye cannot say to the hand, 'I have no need of you'" (1 Cor. 12:21). Both person-centered and group-centered ministry must take into account the other; yet each has a unique emphasis of its own. The family or a ministry cannot ignore one aspect of the Body and ultimately succeed in building the other aspect. We want to build discipleship and fellowship simultaneously.

The Greek word translated "church" in the New Testament is *ecclesia*, which means "the assembly of the called -out ones." As an assembly, the church is a corporate group. As called-out ones, the church is individuals. This description is not limited to the local church. Any group of Christians bonded together in ministry also shares the corporate group aspect and the individual member aspect—or it should.

Key Ingredients in Ministry

My mother, an excellent cook, loves to collect recipes.
When shoe boxes filled with recipes were too much for her
to manage, my dad built a wall of storage drawers for her
recipes. Every once in awhile, when we are having guests
for dinner, Ann Marie will phone my parents and say,
"Calling for Recipe Central," and gets the recipe she
needs.

In all of my life, however, I have never seen my
mother follow a recipe exactly the way it was written; she
adds or leaves out ingredients according to her taste. The
finished product is always personalized, always her. Of
course, certain dishes require essential ingredients.
Chicken a la king without chicken would merely be a la
king!

Ministry is like that. Even though we may personalize
the methods in their various settings so that they create
an infinite variety of ministry styles, methods, and
approaches, there are certain key ingredients to ministry
we must use. Ministry is a practice, not a science, not
exact; it is often ambiguous, often uncertain. Nevertheless, when we use God-given ingredients and trust the
work of the Holy Spirit in us and through us we will see
people grow in life and maturity in Christ.

Three of these key ingredients are *People*, *Principles*,
and *Practice*.

People are the first essential ingredient. It sometimes
seems that pastors and people in ministry believe that program is the purpose of ministry. They look for a program
that has worked elsewhere which they can easily repro-
duce at home. However, people are the ends of ministry;
specifically, enabling the well-being and maturing of those

people in the Body of Christ, both individually and corporately. Jesus recognized that people were central to His ministry. He said, "The Spirit of the Lord is upon Me, because He anointed Me to preach the gospel to the poor. He sent me to proclaim release to the captives, and recovery of sight to the blind, to set free those who are downtrodden, to proclaim the favorable year of the Lord" (Luke 4:18). Paul, also recognized that every person was his purpose for ministry: "And we proclaim Him, admonishing every man and teaching every man with all wisdom, that we may present every man complete in Christ" (Col. 1:28).

Preach the gospel to the poor, release to the captive, recovery of sight to the blind; free the downtrodden, admonish every man, teach with all wisdom every person; present every person complete in Christ—the well-being and maturing of the Body of Christ. People are the reason for ministry. When we understand this, then we can prayerfully assess the needs of those among whom we minister, both the individual needs and the group needs.

The second essential ingredient in ministry is *principles*. A principle is a guide for living, a standard by which we live. A principle is a universal rule of behavior that applies to life in all cultures and all times. For example, in the New Testament we discover the principle of encouragement: "Therefore encourage one another, and build up one another, just as you also are doing" (1 Thess. 5:11). This life-style principle applies to all Christians and Christian fellowships. Whereas people are the ends of ministry, principles are the *means* of ministry. Principles give us the pattern for action that will build people in Christ.

The final ingredient in ministry is *practice*, how we apply principles of ministry in order to best meet the needs of people. For example, to practice the principle of encouragement is to actually say or do that which will encourage a person or a fellowship. An individual expresses the principles of ministry in his or her *life-style*. A group practices the principles of ministry through the life-style of its people and its *program*. A common mistake in ministry is to ignore the first two ingredients of ministry—people and principles, and focus solely on practice, or program. Program, properly done, practices the principles as it ministers to the needs of the people.

A great many recent books, both inside and outside the church, have emphasized principles—principles of management, principles of finance, principles of parenting, principles of all aspects of life. Yet, without an emphasis on the *practice* of principles, principles become only a concise way of stating content simply for the purpose of teaching it. Principles are to be practiced. Without them we act out of our own background, ministering to others in the way we were ministered to. By practicing biblical principles, we will increasingly model the complete ministry of the Master Builder, Jesus Christ.

The key ingredients in ministry can be illustrated by a large glorious fruit tree. The fruit, branches, and leaves represent the "end" or the purpose of the tree's life— mature *people* in the mature Body of Christ. The roots represent the "means" or the *principles* by which nourishment comes to the leaves and fruit—the Scriptures and the indwelling power of the Holy Spirit. The trunk connecting the roots to the fruits symbolizes the *practice* of ministry by a person or a program. We want to know what the fruit or ends of ministry is to be. We want to know the biblical means of ministry, and we must practice the principles.

In the next section of this book we will look at the purpose, principles and practice of building the person in Christ. In Section III we will look at the purpose, principles and practice of building the group. In all we will see four basic patterns you can use to build people in your congregation: (1) person-to-person ministry; (2) the small group; (3) the small-group movement; (4) the discipleship community.

You have a double focus of ministry. As you develop your own understanding of both the ends and the means of ministry, you can learn how to lead individuals in Christian discipleship at the same time you lead your fellowship toward maturity, whether it is a congregation, a women's ministry, a men's fellowship, a youth group, or a home Bible study. I encourage you first to gain an overview of the material, then focus a place to start, whether it is building one person or a small group or a new congregational emphasis, then begin!

SECTION II

ENDS AND MEANS OF MINISTRY
TO THE PERSON

CHAPTER 3

The Finished Project–
A Mature Christian

In our highly mobile society I find that I often have only a few years or even a few months to minister to a person. Jesus had only three years to mature the Twelve so that they could spread the Christian faith. How can we fully use our available time to enable a person to grow in Christ?

Kim plans to be in America three more years before returning to the Far East to a non-Christian environment. Recently, Kim joined your church fellowship. You discover that Kim made a commitment to Christ just six weeks earlier. Coming from an unchurched background, Kim knows very little about the biblical Christian life-style. What would you impart to Kim that could help him continue to walk with Christ as well as mature in Christ after he returns home? How would you impart it?

The question actually is, What are the ends and means of ministry to Kim?

Before we can *prescribe* how to help a person grow toward maturity we must be able to *describe* what a mature Christian is. We need to know what characterizes a growing Christian regardless of his culture, age, gender, or anything else. We need a blueprint, a map, a profile of how we should mature until we conform to the image of Christ, as Paul told the church at Rome (see Rom. 8:29).

The image of Christ is not a rigid mold into which we must force a person within a given time limit until he can be proclaimed "mature." After spending three years modeling and describing a mature person of God to twelve men, Jesus said to His Father, "I glorified Thee on the earth, having accomplished the work which Thou hast given Me to do" (John 17:4). None of the Twelve was fully mature but eleven of them would continue to grow in Christ and manifest their maturity in ministry to others.

We are mature when we are adult, complete, or fully grown. We grow as we move toward maturity. The Bible uses a Greek word, *teleios*, when it speaks of maturity or completion or perfection. The author of Hebrews said, "Leaving the elementary teachings about the Christ, let us press on [swift, energetic movement] to maturity [*teleiotes*]" (Heb. 6:1).[1]

Paul stated his primary purpose in ministry when he said, "And we proclaim Him [Jesus Christ], admonishing every man and teaching every man with all wisdom, that we may present every man complete [*teleios*] in Christ" (Col. 1:28). He told the Corinthians, "Brethren, do not be children in your thinking; yet in evil be babes, but in your thinking be mature [*teleios*]" (1 Cor. 14:20). And to the Ephesians he said, "until we all attain to the unity of the faith, and of the knowledge of the Son of God, to a mature [*teleios*] man, to the measure of the stature which belongs to the fullness of Christ" (Eph. 4:13). James, in his Epistle, said that when his readers encounter trials they would know "that the testing of your faith produces endurance. And let endurance have its perfect [*teleios*] result, that you may be perfect [*teleios*] and complete, lacking in nothing" (1:3-4).

Judging from the frequent use of *teleios* we realize that New Testament writers were concerned about Christian wholeness and maturity.

Teleios, as the end of Christian growth, has both eternal and temporal perspectives. From the eternal perspective, the end of growth is completeness or perfection. From the temporal perspective, the end of growth is well-being and maturity. Absolute *teleios*, when growth is finished, will be reached in eternity. The Body of Christ—as individuals and as a group—will then be perfect, complete, mature, holy and blameless, and sanctified entirely (see Eph. 5:27; Phil. 1:6; 1 Thess. 5:23).

The temporal perspective of *teleios* has to do with the full restoration of God's image in our lives. When we are born again in Jesus this growth process begins, but it is not completed until eternity (see Phil. 1:6; Col. 3:4-10; Luke 6:40). Thus *teleios* is defined by the image of Christ.

Growth and maturation is a process. Although *teleios* is the pattern for our growth, perfectionism as we understand it is not implied. We will not be perfect in this life, but we will continue to grow by grace in the direction of well-being and maturity. Life is dynamic, constantly providing us with new experiences and opportunities for growth if we will learn from and grow in the image of Jesus Christ.

The Birth of the New Self

When you are born spiritually you receive a new self in

Christ and begin to grow your new self in the image of Christ. You have a new life, a new mind, a new life-style. With your new life your "inner person" is able to be filled with His Spirit and renewed day by day (see 2 Cor. 4:16). Your new mind is renewed by the Holy Spirit to know and think according to the image of Jesus Christ. Your new life-style involves all the attitudes and actions that are expressions of Christ's life with you.

We might say these dimensions are "mutually inclusive" since the new life, new mind and new life-style are all essential, inseparable elements of the image of Christ in a person. We may separate them for purposes of discussion and ministry planning; however, they are indivisible in a Christian. Growth in the image of Christ requires that we be concerned with all three dimensions.

The new life. "If any man [or woman] is in Christ, he [and she] is a new creature," said Paul (2 Cor. 5:17). An invisible but real change happens inside you when you put your faith in Jesus Christ. "New Life" is not merely a Christian cliche for church banners—it is real. "We have been buried with Him through baptism into death, in order that as Christ was raised from the dead through the glory of the Father, so we too might walk in newness of life" (Rom. 6:4).

This "newness of life" is not only a change in our thinking or doing; it is a change of our being. At the moment you put your faith in Jesus Christ you pass from death to life (see John 5:24). You are now "justified" and God declares that you are now in right relationship to Him. You are "born again" (John 3:3). You have "a new heart and . . . a new spirit within you" (Ezek. 18:31). God has removed "the heart of stone from your flesh and [has given] you a heart of flesh" (Ezek. 36:26). The old self (the unregenerated life) is dead, having been crucified with

Christ (see Rom. 6:6). The spirit of your mind is now renewable (see Eph. 4:23). You are a child of God (see John 1:12). Your new self delights in the law of God (see Rom. 7:22). The Holy Spirit, with His power to live the Christian life, now lives in you (see Acts 2:38-39).

With regeneration (new birth) and justification you begin the process of growth, known as "sanctification," by which God makes you whole, complete and holy (see 1 Thess. 5:23; Heb. 13:12). During this growth, God will restore His image in you which was distorted in the fall of Adam and Eve and the subsequent effects of sin. He will build your new self in the image of Jesus Christ, a process that will continue throughout your earthly life—at varying degrees of speed—until it is complete in eternity (see Rom. 8:29; 1 Cor. 15:49; 2 Cor. 3:18; Phil. 1:6; Col. 3:10; 1 John 3:2).

If you try merely to "conform" to the life-style of Christ, to live as He lived, you may acknowledge Him as a worthy model, a person to be admired and imitated, as you would a hero. However, even if this were possible—which it is not without the power of the Holy Spirit—you would still be the same person inwardly that you were before you began the "doing." In contrast, if you are born in Christ and grow in His image, you are "becoming" what He is. You must be *transformed* and receive the new life before you can *conform*, grow in knowing Him and His life-style. You cannot grow spiritually until you are born spiritually through faith in Jesus Christ.

When you become a new creation, you become God's temple (see 1 Cor. 6:19-20), His dwelling place filled with His Holy Spirit (see Eph. 5:18). As you mature in Christ you daily open yourself to the filling of the Spirit. When He reveals personal sin, you will continue to grow in the image of Christ as you confess that sin, committing your life anew to Christ and resubmitting yourself to the filling of the Holy Spirit.

This process is done in partnership with God. No one can change the inner self of another person; only God can do that. However, it is everyone's ministry to introduce another person to this new life through faith in Jesus Christ. Then it is our ministry to teach, encourage, and love that person toward spiritual renewal and growth.

Addressing the new life dimension of the new self is a way of saying to a person, "We are not merely concerned with what you know, think, or do, but we are concerned with *you* as a person." Thus, our building program begins with considering how to share effectively the gospel of Jesus Christ that leads to salvation. Next, we consider ways by which the new life may know joy and strength today. We want to give the certain hope which Jesus Christ came to give; the assurance of eternal life and the assurance of Christ's presence and promises in all events of life.

The new mind. "Be renewed in the spirit of your mind, and put on the new self" (Eph. 4:23-24), says Paul. Also, "Be transformed by the renewing of your mind, that you may prove what the will of God is" (Rom. 12.2). He also notes that "we have the mind of Christ" (1 Cor. 2:16). Then Peter says to "gird your *minds* for action" (1 Pet. 1:13, italics added). The new mind is a Spirit-filled mind that involves both knowing and thinking to the point where it governs our doing. The new mind is able to will or choose its attitude and action. It is where we decide to live the new life-style.

When Jesus preached to crowds, as in the Sermon on the Mount, or as He shared with His disciples, His purpose was to impart knowledge to people, knowledge that

He held with conviction, that He wanted others to hold to be true.

The apostle Paul followed this example: "For I received from the Lord that which I also delivered to you" (1 Cor. 11:23; see also 15:3). Paul knew that this knowledge was to be passed on. He said to Timothy, "The things which you have heard from me in the presence of many witnesses, these entrust to faithful men, who will be able to teach others also" (2 Tim. 2:2).

The biblical view of knowledge is "content with conviction," information together with conviction concerning its truth, not mere neutral information or content without value. For example, information says, "The Bible teaches 'God is love.'" Information held with conviction—knowledge—says, "I agree. 'God is love' and He loves me." Information says, "The Bible teaches that 'God is faithful.'" Knowledge says, "Yes, God is faithful to me."

The new mind involves knowing and *thinking*. With the mind of Christ we are to think theologically, that is, we think through and understand life's complexities with a biblically informed mind. Scripture emphasizes over and over the value of wisdom, indicating how important it is for a mind to grasp biblical truth and correctly apply it to a wide variety of life situations.

Even though we have a new life we still experience the sinful influence of the old self. That influence of the old self, though weakening, is still a very real and negative factor in our mortal lives as a Christian. It does not serve God and is unable to understand His Word or obey it. To choose to follow the influence of the flesh is to focus our minds upon the knowledge and life-style that are compatible with the old self (Eph. 2:1-3).

The new mind, on the other hand, is able to receive and believe the knowledge of God. "He who is of God hears the words of God" (John 8:47; see also 1 Cor. 2:14; Heb. 4:2). We respond to this godly knowledge by conforming our life-style more and more to the image of God (see Eph. 4:24-32; Col. 1:9-10). With a new mind in Christ we have the capacity to *choose* the influence we will follow. That is why Paul repeatedly urges us to "be transformed by the renewing of your mind," (Rom. 12:1-2), and "be filled with the Spirit" (Eph. 5:18), and "walk by the Spirit" (Gal. 5:25), and "walk in Him [Christ]" (Col. 2:6). The new life in Christ frees our new minds to choose the new life-style.

Although we cannot bring about renewal in the mind of another person so that he walks according to the Spirit, we can pray that he will be renewed. We can challenge his mind with teaching. We can model and encourage a devotion to the life-style it commends.

The new life-style. Life-style is the way the new self expresses itself in attitude and action; it is practicing the Christian life. The new mind grasps biblical truth and, filled with the Spirit, chooses to live the life-style that is in accord with that truth. The new life-style includes what we do and with whom we do it.

Life-style is our total life expression of who we are as Christians, including our response to the Scriptures. For example, Scripture teaches that because Jesus Christ's essential nature is that of servant, we too are to serve others (see Phil. 2:5-7). Our new self has the essential nature of servant. We serve because we *are* servants and because we *learn* to serve from Scripture. Both being and knowing-thinking can lead to doing.

The biblical word for life-style is "walk" (*peripateo*). More than 30 times in the New Testament, walk refers to our manner of life (see Eph. 4:1; Col. 2:6; 2 John 6). Walk is a marvelous word for life-style, because both have cadence and rhythm, purpose and destination.

Our life-style begins to conform to the image of Christ as we rely upon the Holy Spirit to help us learn and respond to the godly life-style which Scripture reveals. The vital pairing of knowing-thinking and life-style is stressed throughout Scripture. God said to Joshua, "This book of the law shall not depart from your mouth, but you shall *meditate on it* day and night [knowledge and thought], so that you may be careful *to do* [life-style] according to all that is written in it" (Josh 1:8). When Jesus spoke of the wise man who built his house on rock, He characterized the wise man as one who *hears* the word and *does* it. The foolish man only hears the word; he knows it but does not do it (see Matt. 7:24-27). To have a clear grasp of biblical content without taking on the life-style which Scripture demands is to remain immature (see 1 Cor. 3:13; Heb. 5:12-14). Ministry that builds people in Christ does more than impart information; it also encourages and enables those people to specifically apply biblical truth to their daily living.

The Growing Life-Style

We need to understand Christian life-style if we are to help the Body of Christ, individually and corporately, to grow in the image of Christ. If I were to categorize Christian life-style I would say it involves (1) three Life-Style Relationships, (2) Life-Style Marks, and (3) Spiritual Disciplines. These categories help us communicate the Christian life-style to others.

Three Life-Style Relationships of our life-style may be found in the three great commandments which Jesus emphasized in this ministry: (1) the Great Commandment;

(2) the New Commandment; (3) the Great Commission.

The Great Commandment: "'You shall love the Lord your God with all your heart, and with all your soul, and with all your mind.' This is the great and foremost commandment. The second is like it, 'You shall love your neighbor as yourself'" (Matt. 22:27-39). The first part of the commandment has to do with our relationship with the Triune God; the second part, which is also voiced in the New Commandment and the Great Commission, deals with our relationship with others in the Body of Christ and in the world.

The New Commandment: "A new commandment I give to you, that you love one another, even as I have loved you, that you also love one another. By this all men will know that you are My disciples, if you have love for one another" (John 13:34-35). The New Commandment speaks of our relationship with the Body of Christ.

In the Great Commission we see what our relationship with the world is supposed to be like: "Go therefore and make disciples of all the nations, baptizing them in the name of the Father and the Son and the Holy Spirit, teaching them to observe all that I commanded you; and lo, I am with you always, even to the end of the age" (Matt. 28:19-20).

These three commands reveal the life-style of Jesus Christ in three primary relationships beginning with God, His Father. This relationship was the essential feature of His life as recorded in Scripture. The Son's character, attitude, and actions were in perfect harmony with the Father's. To build people in their relationship with God is to build them in faith. It is to build them in their knowledge of God, the Lordship of Jesus Christ, and the filling of the Holy Spirit.

Jesus' second relationship was with His people, the

Body of Christ. "My sheep hear My voice, and I know them, and they follow Me; and I give eternal life to them, and they shall never perish, and no one shall snatch them out of My hand" (John 10:27-28). Jesus was consistently committed to His disciples and those others who followed Him as He sought to encourage and care for them. To build people in their fellowship with one another in Christ is to build them in their unity, interpersonal relationships, and ministry to one another.

The third relationship in Jesus' life-style was with those in the world who were in difficulty and/or those who were outside the faith. He healed the widow of Nain's son (see Luke 7:11-15). He proclaimed good news to the woman of Samaria and led her to a personal faith in Himself (see John 4). To build people in the world is to offer both the good news of Jesus Christ in evangelism as well as to do acts of compassion in service to those not in the fellowship of God's people.

These three Life-Style Relationships—with the Triune God, the Body of Christ, and the world—represent the essential emphases of Jesus' ministry. Ray Ortlund and Chuck Miller call a growing commitment to each of these three relationships the "three priorities."[2] They are very useful in planning ministry to a person or a group since each of the three relationships is a basic facet of the Christian life-style. A ministry that builds people will develop a balanced emphasis on all three.

The Life-Style Marks. The Three Relationships may be expressed in more detail in terms of Life-Style Marks. Eleven basic Life-Style Marks are (1) renewal, (2) worship, (3) Word, (4) prayer, (5) family, (6) fellowship, (7) stewardship, (8) ministry, (9) compassion, (10) evangelism, and (11) work.

To better focus them in our minds, the basic life-style marks can be grouped under the three relationships:

> The Triune God
> > Renewal
> > Worship (including the sacraments)
> > Word
> > Prayer
>
> The Body of Christ
> > Family
> > Fellowship
> > Stewardship
> > Ministry
>
> The World
> > Compassion
> > Evangelism
> > Work

Each Life-Style Mark is an attribute of the Body of Christ, individually and corporately, which expresses the life-style of Jesus: I pray, and we (the church) pray; I show compassion, and we show compassion.

In addition to the eleven life-style marks which may be used as a basic life-style framework for Christian growth, there are additional basic marks or attributes of Christian life-style:

Faith (Rom. 5:1; Heb. 11:1-6)
Hope (1 Thess. 1:3; Heb. 6:19)
Love (1 John 4:16-21)
Confession (1 John 1:9)
Servanthood (Mark 10:43-45)
Holiness (1 Peter 1:14-16)
Righteousness (Matt. 6:33; 2 Tim. 3:16)
Obedience (Phil. 2:8; Heb. 5:8-9)

Humility (Phil. 2:5-8; 1 Pet. 5:6)
Generosity (2 Cor. 9:10-15)
Wisdom (Jas. 1:5-8; the book of Proverbs)
Encouragement (Rom. 15:5; 1 Thess. 5:11)
Steadfastness (1 Thess. 1:3; Jas. 1:1-4)
Forgiveness (Matt. 18:21-35; Col. 3:13)
Fruit of the Spirit (Gal. 5:22-23)

Again, this list is not exhaustive since only the Scriptures as a whole, correctly interpreted, give you the full blueprint for life-style. By grace we ask the Spirit of God to build all of these Life-Style Marks in us and, in turn, to build them into the lives of others through us.

Spiritual Disciplines. A Spiritual Discipline is a practice we consciously put into our own lives to pattern our living and shape our growth in the image of Christ. It is a "chosen habit." The disciplines represent deliberate efforts to build the attributes of the image of Christ into the various contexts of our lives. They are intentional expressions of the means of grace and Christian growth.

For example, a person may seek to grow into these seven personal Spiritual Disciplines of the Christian life:

1. Renewal: daily commitment to Jesus Christ and the filling of the Holy Spirit
2. Word and prayer: daily Bible study and application of its teaching to life and daily prayer, intercession for church, family, those who are ill, nation, authorities, friends, and self
3. Family: regular time with spouse and children, separately and together; attention to matters of spiritual, emotional and physical well-being and attention to family affairs like finances and home maintenance

4. Fellowship: weekly participation in church and a small-group Bible study
5. Stewardship: regular commitment of 10 percent of personal income to the ministry of God's people; the life-style of generosity
6. Ministry: initiatives of care, witness, discipleship, and service offered to meet the needs of people and encourage them to grow in Christ
7. Work: commitment to excellence in relationships and responsibilities in the context of one's work.

When Spiritual Disciplines are kept creatively and consistently, they offer an approach by which a person may grow in the whole image of Jesus Christ. They offer a biblical framework for development of the many other life-style attributes—faith, hope, love, humility, servanthood, and other qualities—that are essential to the Christian growing in Christ's image. *We seek to practice the disciplines consciously until we practice them unconsciously.*

The Three Life-Style Relationships, the Eleven Life-Style Marks, and the Seven Spiritual Disciplines give us a handle on the Christian life-style. They help us know what to build into the lives of the people to whom we minister. They are not meant as standards by which we judge shortcomings and failure, nor are they a new legalism—"If you don't do this and this and this, you are failing." They are positive guides, targets at which to aim. They do not "earn" salvation, since salvation is a gift by the grace of God through our personal faith in Jesus Christ. They do, however, pattern the life-style which those who have salvation should model. As the "ends of ministry" they point the way; they show us where to grow—not simply where we have failed. When we see them this way, they encourage us and show us how to please God.

Stunting growth. It is possible for our progress toward spiritual maturity to be slowed and discipleship diluted. Life "according to the Spirit" moves toward Christian maturity; life "according to the flesh" inhibits spiritual growth.

As a Christian you are clearly free to choose to live according to the Spirit—the life-style that is consistent with your new self. Yet, we so often yield to temptation, even when we know better. The influence of the old self is within us, pulling us to live the old way and act in direct opposition to the new self and the Spirit.

Other inhibitors to growth are discussed by Jesus in the parable of the sower (see Mark 4:3-20); such as the external foes of Satan, affliction, persecution, and the internal foes of worry and materialism. These inner and outer foes of the Spirit pressure us to live according to the "old self." If you want to help people grow up spiritually you must teach them to recognize these foes and equip them to do battle.

You must also teach them how to cope with personal sin and failure: to confess sin and know God's forgiveness (see 1 John 1:9); to be filled with the Spirit (Eph. 5:18); to restore broken relationships (Matt. 5:23-24); and to trust God for help in the midst of trial and temptation (Jas. 1:2-4; 1 Cor. 10:13). Our final confidence in the midst of conflict, be it within or without, comes from the knowledge that "there is therefore now no condemnation for those who are in Christ Jesus" (Rom. 8:1).

The Process of Growth

Personal maturity is a gift and the result of grace. Although we have a role in the maturing process, we recognize that the work is God's.

Discipleship involves all facets of life: spiritual, physical, mental, emotional, and relational. To isolate any one facet is to limit the total maturity of the person. Paul commanded, "Grow up in *all aspects* into Him, who is the head" (Eph. 4:15, itals added).

Discipleship means growing in Christ yourself (becoming a disciple) *and* enabling others to grow in Christ (discipling). Therefore, personal maturity involves responsibility for your own growth and goes one step further to require you to be responsible for the spiritual growth of others.

Discipleship involves a growing awareness of the sin and imperfection in your own life and a simultaneous growing trust in the saving and renewing grace of God which is given to us in Jesus Christ.

Discipleship is a lifelong process. "He who began a good work in you will [continue to] perfect [mature] it until the day of Christ Jesus" (Phil. 1:6). As we do in the physical realm, there are times when we grow slowly and other times when we grow rapidly. Psalm 1 speaks of a tree that bears its fruit *in its season;* even continuous growth does not produce evident fruit all the time. A tree can be healthy even when fruit is not visible.

The evidence that we are growing toward maturity in any arena of a life will be seen in increasing depth and complexity. For example, growth in the maturity of our prayer life will be manifested in an increased knowledge about prayer and ways to pray, and in increased commitment to prayer and the practice of prayer.

Not only will we individually experience times of slow growth and times of fast growth, the rate of spiritual growth will vary among Christians. Once I watched a group of one-year-olds, some of whom were crawling and some walking. A few could speak a few words, but most talked in unintelligible syllables. Some children drank from a cup, while some were still on the bottle or breast. Yet within five years every child in that group would walk, talk, and drink from a cup, because each parent's goal was to enable and encourage the maturing process according to the unique needs and characteristics of the child.

Many factors influence our spiritual growth: age and life stage, family situation, circumstances of life, strengths, weaknesses, motivation and interests. No two Christians will ever be identical, for God has created each of us as unique.

Since there is a difference in the way each person matures, the key to a person-centered ministry is to find aspects of Christian maturity that will allow each person to grow within his or her own limits and abilities. Oswald Chambers said, "Allow the Holy Spirit the same freedom with the next person that He had with you." The extent to which a person grows in the new life, new mind, and new life-style of Jesus Christ are within God's control. Every disciple struggles with the influence of the old self; no one is perfect at new birth. The growing Christian learns to live according to the Spirit by trusting in His power moment by moment, for life.

CHAPTER 4

The Person Under Construction

I like the contemporary Christian chorus, "He's Still Working on Me." God is still working on all of us. But, He uses each of us to help the others of us grow toward His image.

Basically, helping to build another person towards maturity in Christ means that, by God's grace, you:

- enable spiritual formation
- seek to help him learn of Jesus Christ so that he will become His disciple and grow in His image
- build his new life, new mind and new life-style
- encourage him to grow in the Three Relationships, the Eleven Life-Style Marks, and the Spiritual Disciplines.

In the previous chapter we talked about what a mature person is. Now we need to find some biblical guidelines by which we can build that person's new life, new mind, and new life-style in the image of Christ—we need some principles by which to operate. While maturity is the end of ministry, principles are the means of ministry. The principles may be universal, but using them in the setting of your ministry requires preparation and creativity on your part. How you use these principles will vary from person to person and group to group, depending on the needs at the time of ministry.

Jesus had some very definite principles. "And He appointed twelve, that they might be with Him, and that He might send them out to preach." I came across these words in Mark 3:14 when I was looking for some ways to organize the principles of building a person in the image of Christ. The principles in this verse which Jesus used to build people are "with me" and "send them." We will talk about these two principles, among some others, more thoroughly in the next sections.

Defining People-Building Principles

A *principle* is the means or the how to of building people. It is a basic rule of life-style (conduct), how someone should behave or live. A principle is universal in that it applies to human life in all cultures and times.

A *method*, on the other hand, is the specific way we put a principle to use. For example, prayer is one principle for building people. We express this principle through intercessory prayer, prayer partners, and prayer covenants, among others.

Jesus Christ was the Master people-builder. The apostle Paul was also an effective people-builder; so was King

David. We can also learn to build people in the image of Christ. Jesus is our model. "Jesus was going about all the cities and the villages, teaching in their synagogues, and proclaiming the gospel of the kingdom, and healing every kind of disease and every kind of sickness" (Matt. 9:35). Jesus *taught* the good news to His followers in the presence of the disciples; He *modeled* His compassion before His disciples; then He *sent* them out to do the same thing. These three principles are still effective guidelines for building people.

Just as a child matures within the influence of his parents as well as his family as a whole, so too a Christian disciple is influenced not only by the individual who personally ministers to help build him or her, but also by the group of which he or she is a part. We are all influenced by both aspects of the Body of Christ (see fig. 1). This discipling is best done if we organize our action into a set of principles.

Many publications talk about biblical principles and building people. H. H. Horne and A. B. Bruce authored classic works in this area. More recent authors include Robert Coleman, Leroy Eims, Gene Getz, Howard Hendricks, Walter Hendricksen, Charles Miller, James Tozer, Carl Wilson, and others.[1]

I have found it possible to arrange most of the principles of building people under one of five master categories: (1) prayer, (2) care, (3) "with me," (4) Word, and (5) "send them."

The principle of prayer. "To be little with God is to be little for God" (E. M. Bounds). Faithful practice of the principle of prayer is absolutely essential to building people.

Our prayers acknowledge that building people is first and ultimately a work of God in the life of another. In prayer we seek guidance from God concerning, first, who to build. Luke 6 describes how Jesus prayed on the mountain all night, *then* He called His disciples to Him and appointed the Twelve. He selected His apostles from people He knew. As you pray your "prayer of selection," pray over the names of people you already know so that God can direct you to the people on whom you are to focus your person-building ministry.

Jesus not only selected His Twelve, He narrowed the field even further; from the Twelve He selected three: Peter, James and John (Matt. 17:1). As you spend time in prayer over the people you already know, God will lead you to the few you are to focus on, or else He will position those people with you.

Next, when you can name the people you believe that God wants you to build, then your prayers become intercessory. You pray for God's maturing work in them and for God's hand to meet their needs. Many of our prayers for other people are need-oriented: "Lord, help Mary get well . . . . Guide Jo with her daughter . . . . Help John get along with his boss." These prayers for another's well-being are quite appropriate; however, a people-building prayer also asks God to help the person to grow in Christ. Paul told the Colossians about the intercessory prayer which Epaphras prayed on their behalf: "Epaphras, who is one of your number, a bondslave of Jesus Christ, sends you his greetings, always laboring earnestly for you in his prayers, that you may stand perfect [mature] and fully assured in all the will of God" (Col. 4:12, italics added).

People-building through Prayer is a demanding principle because you are responsible for implementing your prayers. Paul felt this responsibility very strongly. He prayed for the Ephesians "that the God of our Lord Jesus Christ, the Father of glory, may give to you a spirit of wisdom and of revelation . . . that the eyes of your heart may be enlightened, so that you may know what is the hope of His calling, what are the riches of the glory of His inheritance in the saints, and what is the surpassing greatness of His power" (Eph. 1:17-19); and also that God "would grant you . . . to be strengthened with power through His Spirit in the inner man . . . [so that you may] know the love of Christ which surpasses knowledge, that you may be filled up to all the fulness of God"(3:16, 19). These are good prayers you may pray for building maturity in a person.

The Care principle. If there is one area of ministry in which the church has been reasonably effective, Care is that area. To apply the principle of Care means that you see another person through difficulty or physical, social, emotional, mental as well as spiritual needs. Its aim is the health or well-being of each person.

Scripture offers many basic principles of caring. Each principle describes a how to of effective care.

- "Jonathan, Saul's son, arose and went to David at Horesh, and encouraged him in God" (1 Sam. 23:16).
  Principle: Encouragement
- "And moved with compassion, [Jesus] stretched out His hand, and touched him, and said to [the leper], 'I am willing; be cleansed'" (Mark 1:41).
  Principle: Touch
- "Confess your sins to one another, and pray for one another, so that you may be healed" (Jas. 5:16).
  Principle: Confession and Prayer.
- "Bear one another's burdens, and thus fulfill the law of Christ" (Gal. 6:2).
  Principle: Burden-bearing

A marvelous expression of the principle of Care is the New Testament concept of the paraclete (*parakletos* in the Greek). A paraclete is one who is called alongside to help. All three members of the Trinity are described individually in Scripture in the role of paraclete. Paul says of God the Father: "Blessed be the God and Father of our Lord Jesus Christ, the Father of mercies and God of all comfort (*paraklesis*)" (2 Cor. 1:3). The Father is a paraclete. John says that "if anyone sins, we have an Advocate (*parakletos*) with the Father, Jesus Christ the righteous" (1 John 2:1); and Jesus says that the Holy Spirit is a paraclete: "I will ask the Father, and He will give you another Helper (*parakletos*), that He may be with you forever" (John 14:16). So too we are paracletes; we too come alongside to help.

Of course, Care is not limited solely to tending a person's wounds. Mark said that Jesus "saw a great multitude, and He felt *compassion* for them because they were like sheep without a shepherd; and He began to *teach* them many things" (6:34, italics added). Today, pastoral care tends to minister to those who suffer in some way; yet, in the broadest sense, caring includes both ministering to someone in need as well as equipping him or her to live a balanced life in Christ.

The With-Me principle. We have already seen that Mark 3:14 depicts two of Jesus' principles. The first: "[Jesus] appointed twelve, that they might be *with Him*" (italics added). Paul speaks of the whole Body of Christ being fitted and held together (see Eph. 4:16). Being with a person is a critical step in building up him or her. Jesus focused on a few to be with Him.

You model Jesus as you invite others to "come with me" to church, to a small group, to ministry. The very word that has come to describe a ministry which many churches embrace—*koinonia*—means fellowship, a shared life. You build people as you invite them to be with you, the intentional sharing of life so that they can learn from you and with you individually as well as from the group. Paul was clear about the Christian's responsibility in modeling Christ: "You also became imitators of us and of the Lord, having received the word in much tribulation with the joy of the Holy Spirit" (1 Thess. 1:6). "The things you have learned and received and heard and seen in me, practice these things; and the God of peace shall be with you" (Phil. 4:9). "For you yourselves know how you ought to follow our example, because we did not act in an undisciplined manner among you" (2 Thess. 3:7). "Be imitators of me, just as I also am of Christ" (1 Cor. 11:1). "Brethren, join in following my example, and observe those who walk according to the pattern you have in us" (Phil. 3:17). The only way another person can imitate, practice, follow, and observe is by being with you.

People naturally imitate and emulate one another. If your Christianity is full of power and glorifies God, others will model your Christian life, knowledge and life-style. Of course, you know you are not perfect. Even Paul was not a perfect model; he frequently confessed his shortcomings. But he modeled humility in that he confessed his sins and weaknesses to others. So you should never let the fact that you have not yet reached perfection (complete maturity) deter you from asking others to be with you so that you can model the faith which you have already, and so that both of you can learn from the group as a whole.

In the With-Me principle your own Christian life, knowledge, and life-style serve as *a* blueprint; Jesus Christ is *THE* blueprint. You are only a pattern of Christian discipleship, expressed in accord with your own personality, style and characteristics. For example, what you may learn about the principle of Prayer from me would be my devotion to regular praying. How you pray, your manner of expression, your style, however, will be you rather than me.

During With-Me time you can initiate conversation that will build the other person in Christ. Jesus frequently asked questions of His disciples and others so that He could lead them to new insights, such as He did on the road to Caesarea Philipi when Peter declared that He was the Christ.

An important aspect of the With-Me principle is that you focus on the few. Although large numbers of people may be with you in worship services or Bible class, you cannot effectively build everyone who is with you on a personal basis. While Jesus ministered to many, He focused on a few—the Twelve—and gave particular attention to the inner three, Peter, James and John. So, too, you must model Christ by focusing on a few, finding ways to get them to be "with me" in fellowship, study, leisure and ministry.

Look for creative ways to be with the few you seek to build in Christ. If you go to minister—speak to a group, visit someone in the hospital, share your faith, attend a seminar out of town—don't go alone. Just being together in ministry will give the other person an opportunity to catch a vision for ministry rather than simply being told to "go minister." But don't limit your With-Me time to the "religious" aspect of your life. Have your disciple share your life at an evening meal, a game of golf, or other leisure activities with you and your family.

During your With-Me time you may talk about your personal lives, families, the nation, or the ministry at hand. You will pray together. You will naturally and consciously bring up matters of faith and life. God will use this time to bond you together as personal friends and will stimulate both of you to grow in Christ.

The principle of the Word. "All Scripture is inspired by God and profitable for teaching, for reproof, for correction, for training in righteousness; that the man of God may be adequate, equipped for every good work" (2 Tim. 3:16-17). We build people with the Word of God by helping them grasp its meaning and apply it to their lives. We build as we equip people to feed themselves, give them skills, and encourage them to practice regular Bible study on their own.

"Like newborn babes, long for the pure milk of the word, that by it you may grow in respect to salvation" (1 Pet. 2:2). The Word is our content, the gospel of Jesus Christ, the whole counsel of God. It is everything we need to hear in order to grow in Jesus Christ. We need to share not only our knowledge of the *content* of Scripture but also the *skills* which are needed to live the new life in Christ. Jesus said the man who built his house on a rock was the wise man who heard the Word and *did* it.

How do you help another person "do" the Word? I can think of three ways: (1) offer to guide Bible study in humility, "Let's discover together what Scripture says," not "Sit down, I'm gonna give you the truth;" (2) relate the passage you are studying to the real needs of the other person; (3) share what excites you in Scripture. Of course, you need to regularly review the basics of Christian faith and life along with whatever you are currently excited about.

The form of Bible study that is most effective in leading a person to act upon what he hears is called inductive Bible study. This method asks three basic questions of the text being studied: (1) What does it say? (the observation step); (2) What does it mean? (the interpretive step); (3) What do I do? (the application step). By inductively studying passages of Scripture, God through His Holy Spirit will mature both you and the person you are building.

The Send-Them principle. The second half of the fourteenth verse of Mark 3 is: "Jesus appointed twelve . . . that He might send them out to preach." To send is one of the key verbs in the Bible. Whereas the word *disciple* means literally "one who learns," the word *apostle* means "one who is sent." Jesus called the Twelve His apostles (see Luke 6:13). From the very beginning they understood that their destiny was to be sent. Jesus said, "As the Father has sent Me, I also send you" (John 20:21).

Sending is essential to an equipping ministry, for in sending we take the step of sharing ministry with others. Just as a parent releases a child into adulthood to assume the full demands of an adult, so we will release or send the people we are building. Your objective is not to gather a group of fawning students to admire you and be with you forever; rather, it is to build them to a point of self-responsibility and a willingness to care for others, then to release them—send them—and encourage them to go. Sometimes, through prayer and laying on of hands, as the church in Antioch did with Paul and Barnabas (see Acts 13:3-4), you may formally send a person to his or her own ministry. At other times you may simply encourage a person to have a personal ministry without saying anything about sending.

You prepare people to be sent when you help them to develop a heart for others. Matthew 9:36 reports that, after preaching, teaching, and healing, Jesus saw the multitudes and "felt compassion for them, because they were

distressed and downcast like sheep without a shepherd."
Jesus imparted His concern for other people and helped
them to see those who needed a shepherd. He told them,
"The harvest is plentiful, but the workers are few. Therefore beseech the Lord of the harvest to send out workers
into His harvest" (Matt. 9:37-38). Those who need a
shepherd are the families, neighbors, and co-workers of
the one you are building. Some of these people who touch
their lives are the "distressed and downcast," some worn
down, and some thrown down by the events in their lives.

Another way to help a person develop a heart for ministry is to involve him in opportunities to use his gifts in
the practice of ministry. This, of course, assumes you and
the person you seek to build have already studied in the
Word about the spiritual gifts which God gives to all of His
followers. Understanding the gifts and finding the one or
ones he has, then seeking a place in the Body to practice
his gifts, is a valid way to help the person you are preparing for ministry.

Sending out to minister does not have to have geographical implications. When Jesus said, "As the Father
has sent Me, I also send you," it sounds as though Jesus
was sending His apostles to the whole known world, but a
long time passed before some of them left Jerusalem. Yet,
they did assume the responsibility for ministry; they did
continue to build people.

You can impart a vision for personal ministry into the
consciousness of the person you are building by using the
principles we have already discussed: *pray* that he or she
may catch the vision, beseeching the Lord for workers as
He commanded; you can demonstrate that you *care* for
those who are "distressed and downcast" and let him or
her see how you act upon your concern while "*with me*".
And, of course, the *Word* has many passages that exhort

us to share our faith, care for the poor, helpless, widowed, orphaned, deceived and misguided. No single sermon, occasional "minute for mission" during a worship service, or brief article in a church newsletter will begin to do the job alone. You must emphasize to your disciple that a personal ministry is an integral part of growing in the image of Christ. You need to constantly encourage the few to recognize the "distressed and downcast," the "sheep without a shepherd" so they will pray, "Lord, how may I serve these people on your behalf?"

It is in the principle of sending that you greatly increase your own impact for Christ in the world. Instead of ministering by yourself, now you and the sent learner *both* minister to people. This is the principle of multiplication. "And the things which you have heard from me in the presence of many witnesses, these entrust to faithful men, who will be able to teach others also" (2 Tim. 2:2).

We can group a great many other principles of ministry under the five master people-building principles.

Prayer
1. Select (Lord, who do you want to be with me/us?) Luke 6:12
2. Intercede (prayers in behalf of those with me/us) 1 Thessalonians 1:2
3. Assess (Lord, what are the needs of those with me?) 1 Corinthians 3:2

Care
1. Be a paraclete (encouragement, comfort, exhortation—come alongside to help) 1 Samuel 23:16
2. Touch, Mark 1:41
3. Confess and Pray, James 5:16

4. Bear burdens, Galatians 6:2

With-Me
1. Focus on a few, Luke 6:13
2. Invite personally, Matthew 4:19
3. Be "with me" in a small group, John 18:2
4. Be "with me" in ministry, Matthew 14:19
5. Model (the Christian life), Philippians 4:9
6. Minister mutually, Proverbs 27:17.
7. Correct and make accountable, 2 Timothy 4:2
8. Be vulnerable, Philippians 2:25
9. Challenge and motivate, 1 Thessalonians 2:11
10. Have fun, John 2:2
11. Eat together, Acts 2:46
12. Go on retreats, Mark 6:30-32

Word
1. Impart knowledge (the content of Scripture), Acts 20:20, 27
2. Transfer concepts (teach concepts in such a way that the learner can pass them to others), Matthew 13:3
3. Build a life-style (the Three Life-style Relationships, Life-Style Marks, and Spiritual Disciplines), Matthew 7:24
4. Demonstrate, do and review (tell and show how to practice some aspect of life-style; let them do it; review the results), Luke 8:1; 9:1-2, 10
5. Repeat and run deep (teach a congregation or fellowship about a concept, then repeat the teaching in greater depth with a few, just as Jesus taught the parable of the sower to the Twelve), Mark 4
6. Expose to experience (interpret life's events with biblical perspective), John 9:3

7. Teach, Acts 2:42

Send-Them
1. Find a ministry, Mark 3:14-15
2. Let your learners go, Matthew 28:19-20
3. Multiply, 2 Timothy 2:2

Learning to use the five basic principles of building people will open up many sub-principles and a myriad of methods or specific ways to practice the principle. To reduce the master principles even further, we may view building people as involving the practice of *care* and *discipling* (Prayer, With, Me, Word, Send Them). In the church these are frequently represented by the ministries of pastoral care and Christian education. Yet, these principles are not reserved for committees and programs. They are intended to be practiced by people as part of their daily Christian life-style. To build people as disciples, to care for them and to equip them to disciple and to care for others was at the heart of the people-building ministry of Jesus Christ.

Applying the Principles

These principles are actually generic tools we use to lovingly influence others to grow in Christ. You may use them to build one other person; your congregation may use them to build several people or even another congregation. As "iron sharpens iron, so one man sharpens another" (Prov. 27:17). Some of the tools you will use all of the time; others only at special times. For example, you pray the prayer of selection when you ask God to show you the next Christian He wants you to build; but you pray prayers of intercession during the entire time you are concerned for the well-being of that person (possibly for the rest of your life).

Once God has led you to the person(s) you are to build, you do not necessarily announce, "You are my disciple." Such a remark could insult the person if he is older than you or your peer. When you build people you, like Jesus, are their servant. Yet, at times a formal teacher-student relationship is appropriate. But whether formal or informal, building another person is always mutual, each sharpening the other. Since you are both pilgrims in the journey of faith you are, as D. T. Niles said, "Like one beggar telling another beggar where to find bread."

It is important for you to know that, by God's grace, you can enable and encourage another person to grow by making available the tools and information of growth and by modeling the Christian life-style. Even though the principles are God-given means of grace and growth, they do not guarantee growth in anyone. The parable of the sower indicates this (see Mark 4). Unfortunately, some will "fall away," become hostile and/or divisive in the church. Jesus had Judas. Spiritual growth in each individual will ultimately come from his or her own desire to grow and from the work of the Holy Spirit within that person, both of which are beyond your control.

Building another person in Christ is certainly not cloning. It is not forcing a person into rigid, identical expressions of new life, biblical knowledge, or life-style. Rather, building another person means that you impart essential renewal, knowledge and life-style, enabling and allowing the person to express his or her Christian walk in ways that are consistent with Scripture and with all the diversity of the God-given personality, age, background, and experience.

This chapter has focused on principles rather than

detailed plans because biblical principles of building people are eternal. As you use them in your own unique way, in your own unique circumstances, they will become a part of your life-style and the life-style of the person you build. Through them God will build Christian maturity.

CHAPTER 5

Person-to-Person Ministry

A few years ago I was running around an indoor track at Purdue University as part of a noon exercise class. I was really out of shape and was struggling to finish my last lap when a hand slapped me on the back. It was Steve, an acquaintance of mine from church.

Knowing that God "positions" us with people so that we might develop friendships with them and minister to them, I decided to run one more lap alongside Steve. We chatted about the weather and things in general. As we were finishing that lap, Steve said, "You know, Stan, I'm a salesman, and most nights I have little to do when I'm out of town staying in motel rooms. Lately I've been reading the Bible, and I must say that God is doing something in my life."

I have to admit that a part of me wondered why God waited until I had already run six laps before positioning

Steve in my life that day. But with joy I was able to say, "That's wonderful Steve. What has God been doing?" And we ran another lap!

Eventually we met for lunch and made a prayer covenant, agreeing to pray for each other every day for 30 days. Steve went with me to call on those who had visited our church, and he learned to share his faith in Christ in sensitive yet effective ways. God used our time together to build both of us in Christ through the exercise of the three ingredients of ministry: people, principles, and practice. We focused on our needs as people and we practiced the biblical principles of ministry to build each other in a variety of settings. This was an instance of one-on-one or person-to-person ministry.

This chapter will introduce practical ways to use the ingredients of ministry person-to-person. We will consider how you can Assess a Person's Needs, Practice the Principles, Make "With-Me" Time Effective, and Build Members of Your Own Family.

Almost everything described in this chapter which deals with ministering to one person at a time can also be used effectively in a small group of three, four or even ten people. The Small Group allows enough intimacy that each member can get as much, or more, content and encouragement time as he would if the group leader met with him alone. Also, regular meetings of the Small Group make it easier to schedule. One-on-one ministry, especially ministry by appointment, requires a great deal of initiative on the part of the leader. We will discuss the small group more thoroughly in chapter 10.

Assess a Person's Needs

Since *people* is the first ingredient in ministry, you begin your person-to-person ministry with an assessment of a person's spiritual (and physical) needs. Assessing needs simply means you seek to understand the person's situation before you minister to him. In doing this, however, you must be careful not to come across as someone who is super spiritual. Be aware of the log in your own eye as you seek to assess the needs in another person.

I say "assessing" rather than "evaluating" because no sense of judgment or failure is involved. We assess in order to serve people, not to judge them. To assess needs and not address them can turn into judgmentalism, not to mention gossip. "Aha! He's not a Christian," or "Umm, no commitment to fellowship, I see!" To assess, then address, those needs is ministry.

We need the utmost sensitivity and confidentiality to determine where a person is in general well-being and in discipleship. We know that our insight is limited. We prayerfully seek God's guidance in determining how best to build a particular individual. Assessment allows you to participate actively and appropriately in other people's lives.

Assessment is best done in a time of prayer. This is another significant way to use the master person-building principle of *Prayer*. Ask God about this person He has positioned you with. He knows him or her already and can enlighten you concerning his or her needs.

Since the purpose of ministry is his well-being and discipleship, you could begin your prayers by asking God about the person's all-around well-being. "Lord, is it well with Charlie? This basic question leads to many others. Does he need his self-esteem built up? Is he having any relationship problems with anyone? How is his health? Is he going through pain, grief, anxiety, or insecurity?"

Then, regarding his discipleship, you could pray, "Lord, is Charlie growing in discipleship the way you want

him to grow?" Again, this basic question suggests several
more: "Is his new life maturing as it should be through
faith in Jesus Christ and the filling of the Holy Spirit? Is he
growing in the new mind by learning and understanding
Scripture? Is he growing in Christian life-style through the
Three Relationships, the Life-Style Marks, and Spiritual
Disciplines?"

While you are praying, assess yourself as you assess
Charlie. "Lord, is it well with me? Am I growing in discipleship?" What you seek to offer to others, you ask to
grow in yourself.

How effective your ministry is to Charlie will depend in
part on the answers you receive to these assessment
questions. Even mentioning these needs in prayer will
heighten your sensitivity to Charlie's needs. Essentially,
you want to help him personally to grow *and* help him bond
to a fellowship group. For example, if you soon realize that
Charlie is not committed to Christ, you may look for an
opportunity to share the gospel in a sensitive, clear way,
or you may simply share how Christ has changed your own
life. If he is not committed to fellowship with the Body of
Christ, you may invite him to go with you to a worship service and, if appropriate, to a Small Group fellowship. You
may share Acts 2:42-47 and discuss the value of being
with other Christians on a regular basis, with those who
are also on their walk of faith. If he needs to begin his own
ministry in serving others, ask him to go along with you as
you minister to someone else. If he has an apparent or
expressed physical, spiritual, emotional, mental or social
need, you could either find ways to meet the need personally or else connect him with someone who can help.

The Content Chart in Appendix A will help you discern
Charlie's discipleship needs and whether he is able to handle only basic knowledge and skills or if he is ready for

intermediate or advanced knowledge and skills.

Of course, assessing Charlie's needs does *not* mean you will be 100 percent accurate or complete. However, even getting a partial grasp of Charlie's situation will help you in your ministry to him. As you try to be alert to Charlie's needs in order to help him mature toward the image of Christ, God will build and bless you both.

Practice the Principles

There are many ways to practice each principle. Three very common ministry opportunities are (1) the ongoing personal relationship with the person; (2) the entry of a new person into a fellowship group; (3) ministry by appointment in which you and another person meet together for the express purpose for study and spiritual growth.

Pat leads a small group, which act as a corporate people builder that uses Prayer, Care, With-Me, Word and Send-Them principles. As leader, Pat cannot focus one-on-one with all 10 people in his group, it would take too much time. So, just as Jesus focused on Peter, James and John, Pat has decided to narrow his focus, beginning with just one person—Charlie. Pat will do five things (at least) in a person-building focus on Charlie.

First, Pat will pray for and with Charlie on a regular basis. They will make a Thirty-Day Prayer Covenant (explained in the next section) where they will each pray for the other. Pat will pray that God will develop in Charlie a heart for Himself, His people, and His world, and that He will meet Charlie's needs.

Second, Pat will offer care and encouragement appropriate to Charlie's needs. He will share what is happening in his personal life and encourage Charlie to share with him. In this way they will be able to see how God works to answer their needs.

Third, Pat will find ways (in Small Group, over lunch, in recreation and socially) to be with Charlie whenever possible. Their time together is the key to a personal relationship and will help them both to grow in Christ.

Fourth, Pat will share Scripture with Charlie. This sharing is not necessarily a formal teaching time but is more like, "Wow! I was encouraged by this passage today! Let me share it with you and maybe it will encourage you too."

Fifth, Pat will encourage Charlie to develop a heart for ministering to others. The entry of a new person into their fellowship provides a good ministry opportunity. Perhaps John, a visitor to the worship service, would be someone Charlie could relate with. So, exercising the With-Me principle, Pat takes Charlie over to meet John. They invite him to attend their Small Group meeting with them. They may phone John or have lunch with him, just to develop their new friendship. Little or nothing may be said of Jesus Christ, but both Pat and Charlie will pray that God will develop in John a commitment to Jesus Christ and to His people.

At the next fellowship meeting, Pat and Charlie focus on John again. Perhaps this time Pat and Charlie will separate, each taking another person to meet John so that John's network of relationships continues to expand.

Here we see Pat equipping Charlie to use the principles of building people. *Prayer*: Pat and Charlie prayed for John. Soon they will seek to pray *with* John as well as for him. *Care*: Pat and Charlie introduced John to the small group and helped to make him comfortable in it. They introduced John to others in the group and they will seek to minister to whatever needs they become aware of in

John. *With-Me*: Charlie was invited to be with Pat to talk to John. He saw Pat focus on John. Eventually, Pat will transfer responsibility for John's ministry onto Charlie. *Word*: What Pat and Charlie say to John will depend on their assessment of what is appropriate. They may share the gospel, invite John to come to their Small Group again, or provide some other ministry to John, fulfilling the *Send-them* master principle.

We may practice the principles in both informal and formal disciple-building relationships. To pray daily for another person to grow in Christ, to spend time with each other, to share the Word are excellent ways close friends may effectively encourage one another. In this way, the principles become a part of our *life-style* as we learn to exercise them almost without thinking about them. On the other hand, to be the most consistent and effective in building another person, ministry by appointment offers a more formal use of the principles as we meet on a planned and regular basis with someone in order to study and apply the Word and to grow together in our walk with Christ.

Make "With-Me" Time Effective

The basic question most people ask about person-to-person ministry is, "What do we do when we are *with* each other?" Just how do you actually practice Care, With-Me, Word, Send-Them and further Prayer principles when you are ministering to another person?

Whether you meet the other person for a casual lunch or a more formal study appointment, a conversation pattern you could follow that touches on both well-being and discipleship is the Discipleship Triangle (see fig. 1). Each conversational topic advances the personal relationship between you and the other person and between both of you and God. The order of these topics, Word—Share—People—Prayer, is not important, nor is it necessary for every topic to be covered in any one given conversation. The Triangle simply offers a pattern to help you recall the elements of conversation that will promote growth in Christ. Learn the topics of the Discipleship Triangle by repeating them several times aloud: "Word, Share, People, Prayer." (They even rhyme, which makes memorizing easier.)

The Discipleship Triangle

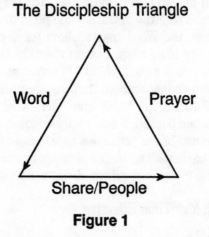

Word   Prayer

Share/People

Figure 1

Word, of course, employs the principle of the Word. As you share Scripture with each other you both grow in commitment to the Triune God and closer to each other. In a formal study appointment in which you and the other person meet for the express purpose of study and Christian growth, you may actually teach from Scripture, perhaps using a study workbook as a guide. In informal times, such as before or after a group meeting or over supper at home, the "Word" portion of the Discipleship Triangle suggests a much more casual sharing of Scripture, often in the context of a personal testimony about how God revealed another aspect of Himself in an experience you had during the past week.

You do not share Scripture to impress others with your biblical knowledge; you share because you are excited about what you are learning for yourself. "I was so encouraged by a verse in Psalm 37 I read this morning during my quiet time. God really spoke to me concerning my anxiety about work. 'Commit your way to the Lord, trust also in HIm, and He will do it.'" By approaching the ministry principle of the Word in this way, not only do you offer an insight from Scripture as a joy in your own life-style rather than "here is a lesson I prepared for you," but you also model that you are committed to a quiet time wherein you study the Bible.

If Louise has expressed a specific need that can be easily answered by Scripture, you can share the appropriate Bible passages which the Holy Spirit reveals to you. For example, if she is struggling with a major decision in her life, you could share verses like Proverbs 3:5-6: "Trust in the Lord with all your heart, and do not lean on your own understanding. In all your ways acknowledge Him, and He will make your paths straight." Use the Bible to inform, encourage, direct and, when appropriate, to confront. (Learn to use a concordance to help you find verses that will minister.) Never use the Bible as a club to punish or put down a person you are trying to build.

There are several approaches to discussing Scripture during the "Word" portion of the Discipleship Triangle:

1. Study the next section of the guide or Bible book you are going through together.
2. Assess the current needs of the other person.
3. Share whatever God is using in Scripture that is

exciting to you and/or the person you are building.
4. Refer to the Content Chart in Appendix A.

Whether you choose a biblical passage or whether you
go with whatever is in the next part of the Scripture guide
you are going through, God will help you adjust the content to meet the needs of the person you are building.

Share, the next leg of the Discipleship Triangle,
employs the principles of With-Me and Care. During this
time you share recent life experiences with each other,
both the *blessings*—where you have seen God at work
during the past week, and also the *needs*—where you
want to be prayed for. This is a time of caring for each other's well-being. Your commitment to each other and to
God will grow as you become involved in each other's personal lives. The more of yourselves you disclose to each
other, the deeper your relationship will be.

Be careful, if you are using a workbook or study guide
during your study appointment, that the structured lesson
does not take up most of your time together. Purposefully
keep the Triangle in balance and leave time for sharing of
your personal lives. Remember, your personal friendship
is as valuable to your mutual growth as is the study and
discussion of Scripture. Don't feel you have to cover "all
the lesson" during one appointment. You can continue the
Bible portion next time. Of course, the reverse is also
true. You could spend all your time over lunch sharing
friendships so that discussion of the Word will never enter
the conversation. The solution here is to spend regular
time in the Word so that it bears fruit like the seed sown on
good ground (see Luke 8:15).

People in the Discipleship Triangle refers to discussion

about others to whom you both will minister, either separately or together. These people may be family members, fellow workers, neighbors, or others in your fellowship group. As you discuss them—without gossip or judgment—your concern is to teach how to assess: "What does Mrs. Jones need?" "How can we build up Sharon during this time of disappointment?" As you focus together on a third person and talk about specific needs in order to minister to him or her, you will develop in the person you are building a heart for other people, a knowledge that "I am sent to serve."

Think of the people who benefit by this leg of the triangle: the person who is the target of the conversation will be blessed as you pray for him and/or supply a need; the person you are building up will be blessed because of the opportunity to see service in action; and you will be blessed because you learn to trust God more as you see Him act on His Word.

Prayer in the Discipleship Triangle refers to the prayers you pray with the other person. It is amazing how God will not only draw two people together in deep relationship, but He will also answer their prayers for help when they pray together. Jesus said, "If two of you agree on earth about anything that they may ask, it shall be done for them by My Father who is in heaven. For where two or three have gathered together in My name, there I am in their midst" (Matt. 18:19-20). Two together can know the presence of Christ and His power.

Sometimes it take courage for you to suggest that the two of you have a word of prayer. Amazingly, most people are delighted to pray with you but are afraid to bring it up. The invitation to have prayer together is by no means something only pastors do. It is the wonderful privilege of every Christian. If you are both unfamiliar with conversational "aloud" prayer, you might suggest, "I'll be happy to lead us in prayer. If you want to say something aloud, fine. If not, it's OK."

You may extend your prayer relationship by making a "Thirty-Day Prayer Covenant." To make such a covenant, you each agree to pray one specific prayer for the other every day for thirty days. Unless you have a specific need, you could pray one of the prayers the apostle Paul speaks of: Ephesians 3:16-19; Colossians 1:9-12; 1Thessalonians 3:11-13. A Prayer Covenant is an outstanding way to build one another in Christ.

The Discipleship Triangle topics conform to the Three Life-Style Relationship commitments of strengthening mutual ties to (1) the Triune God—*Word, Prayer*; (2) each other in Christian fellowship—*Share*; (3) the world in ministry—*People*.

After every time you meet together, whether informally or in a study appointment, plan your next step. It is crucial that there be a next step, another time to meet, a phone call, lunch together, a note in the mail, a game of golf, an invitation to a Small Group, supper in your home. Not to follow through on a next step is to miss an opportunity to build the person.

Don't be afraid to challenge a person. Give Charlie and Louise all they will take. If Charlie will study the Bible one hour a week, great! If Louise can only handle 10 minutes, terrific! Be enthusiastic. If he will memorize Scripture with you, wonderful! If she shares her faith with a fellow worker, exciting!

Be creative. Look for ways to offer encouragement to grow in the Life-Style Marks. Don't be judgmental or critical if Charlie messes up. Offer patient encouragement the way the Holy Spirit does. Be vulnerable and confess your own failures and shortcomings. Look for new ways to use the People-Building Principle of With-Me. Not only will you see God build people through you, but you will also mature in Christ.

Minister to Your Own Family

All of the principles of building people have a natural place for expression in the family. Although many families unconsciously practice the principles to some degree— praying and caring for one another, sharing with each other, the family environment can be greatly enhanced when People-Building Principles are consciously and continuously practiced.

Practicing the principle of Prayer leads a parent to pray daily for the well-being and growth in Christian discipleship of Cindy and Matthew. That way, Cindy and Matthew are taught and encouraged to pray daily too. Parents show Care in many ways with each other and with their children. Husband and wife plan a With-Me time each week to strengthen their relationships. One parent can take one child at a time for a special With-Me time. Adults often pass up opportunities to include their children "I am going to the grocery store. Do you want to go with me?" Or, "I have to run over to the office, do you want to go with me?" With-Me time offers opportunities to build the other up.

There are so many demands on families today that parents must be very deliberate in finding effective ways to build the Word into family life. Some families read and discuss the Bible at bedtime or breakfast. You could start the day with a Scripture verse to memorize. Play Christian music records or tapes. Once in a while, include your child in your own personal prayer and Bible study time and let him or her hear you pray. This is an ideal way to model a life-style and can lead into exciting times to discuss spiritual things. Much better than throwing life-style principles at them as you would the daily duty roster.

A parent whose spouse does not have interest in spiritual things must be especially creative in finding appropriate ways to bring the Word into the lives of children without offending the marriage partner.

The Send-Them principle is one of the most exciting for children to learn. It teaches them to build their friendships. Bringing food to church for Thanksgiving and Christmas baskets, and then helping to deliver the baskets to needy families is a great adventure to a child. Adopting a child in Kenya or South America for a small amount of money each month, then sending letters and cards—and getting a reply back, opens up world missions to young children. These things that can be taught when your children are young, are experiences they will remember as an expression of ministry.

The principles of building people are universal. Find ways to practice them in your family and watch them uplift and encourage each person as you participate in joyful opportunities.

There is an art to building people, one which you can learn and master. An artist uses basic principles of painting as he puts brush to canvas; yet every artist and every art work is unique. As you build another person in the image of Christ, he or she will learn from you. But the Master Teacher is Jesus Christ, and the person will conform to His image as you let go and the Holy Spirit takes hold.

SECTION III
ENDS AND MEANS OF
MINISTRY TO THE GROUP

Building the Fellowship

One evening I sat near Tom Saxon, minister of music, as he directed an orchestra in Polenc's "Gloria." As I watched the musicians from the conductor's perspective, I suddenly realized that the orchestra is a marvelous illustration of the Body of Christ. In order for an orchestra to be complete, or mature, it must have:

PERSONAL ASPECT
    Mature musicians
        People with growing musical skills.
CORPORATE ASPECT
    Leadership
        The conductor who leads the group
    Bonding factors
        Every musician is committed to the orchestra

(unity); every musician's music is in proper
relation to the others (relationships); every
musician has a particular role in which to serve
the orchestra (ministry)

Nested structure

Strings (violins, violas); woodwinds (flutes,
clarinets); percussion (drums, cymbals); brass
(trumpets, trombones)

Knowledge and life-style

The conductor and musicians have a common
knowledge of music and together express the
life-style of an orchestra by playing a symphony.

Every musician has a personal life-style or role, yet
the sound of the whole is the sum of *all* the parts, a corporate life-style. In a similar way, the Body of Christ has a
personal aspect with maturing persons, and a corporate
aspect that bonds the individuals together.

In Section II we discussed how to build a *person* in the
image of Christ. In this section we will address the corporate aspect of the Body of Christ or how to build a *fellowship* in the image of Christ. If spiritual formation is our aim
for each person, fellowship formation is our aim for each
group.

The *teleios* (remember that Greek word for maturing?), or the end of ministry is the same for a Small Group
or Congregation as it is for the individual: to be conformed
to the image of Christ.

Suppose you are about to walk into a room to lead out
in the formation of a new Christian fellowship. You open
the door and see 30 people sitting there, chatting with one
another. You soon learn that not only is every person a
stranger to the rest but they cover a wide spectrum of
Christian maturity. How will you go about creating a *koino-*

nia, a mature Christian fellowship from this group of strangers who have very little in common? What will be the characteristics of such maturity? How will you build these 30 people into the image of Christ?

Whether the "group" is a congregation, a women's ministry, couple's fellowship, or Small Group Bible study, you need to help each person bond to the group and become a functioning and accepted member of the group. Once the group has formed (and continues to form), a leader will guide the whole into the dimensions of new life, new mind, and new life-style.

There are three basic requirements to forming a fellowship: (1) capable leadership, (2) what Paul describes as becoming "fitted together," and (3) what I call "nesting." Each of these aspects grow in strength and effectiveness as the group grows together in the image of Christ.

Developing Capable Leadership

A leader is someone who knows where he or she is going (a purpose) and has others going along with him (a people) on the way (a plan). In ministry, your purpose—where you are going—is to build the well-being and maturity of each person individually and the group as a whole. A leader gives full expression to the With-Me principle.

Every leader should remember that the Head, the primary leader of the Body, is Jesus Christ Himself: "But speaking the truth in love, we are to grow up in all aspects into Him, who is the *head, even Christ, from whom* the whole body, being fitted and held together by that which every joint supplies, according to the proper working of each individual part, causes the growth of the body for the building up of itself in love" (Eph. 4:15-16, italics added). Jesus offers the ministry of leadership to the Body and enables it to grow to maturity. He said, "*I* will build *My* church" (Matt. 16:18). Human leaders, the undershepherds, get their instructions from Him.

Christian leadership has several responsibilities: to equip individual Christians for their personal ministries (Eph. 4:11-12); to shepherd the Body (1 Pet. 4:1-2; Jas. 5:14-15; Acts 6:2-4); to guard the Body from division (Acts 20:28-30); and to build the maturity of the Body (Eph. 4:11-13; Col. 1:28).

In order to fulfill these responsibilities, a leader or leadership team must attend to three tasks: leading, discipline, house management.

Leaders must *lead*! They must know where they are going by utilizing a workable planning process (see chap. 8), and must bring people along with them. Christian leadership often majors on preaching/teaching and pastoral care and minors in leadership. Seminaries offer little by way of leadership and management training; yet in countless cases, ineffective ministries are the result of poor leadership and management skills.

A leader at times will have to offer *correction and discipline*. There are occasions when a person or group may act in a manner so unbecoming to Christ or to His people, or in a manner so hurtful and divisive to the Body, that a leader must sensitively, yet effectively, act in order to preserve the well-being of the group.

The third area leaders have to be concerned about, *house management*, includes many crucial support aspects of Body life such as finances—the stewardship or sound management of all funds and possessions of the fellowship; facilities—the management of building and property; materials—supplies such as books, food for community gatherings, hymnals, etc. In a Small Group, the leader may personally attend to all these house management functions. In larger groups and in a Congregation they are divided among people or ministry area committees.

Leadership and ministry are best done in teamwork. One person cannot build crowds of people to any depth. Barnabas exemplified this when he built his ministry team. He recruited Paul when the church in Antioch began to increase (Acts 11); that team continued to expand as the church grew (Acts 13:1). Paul began many of his letters by naming a team, such as Paul, Silvanus, and Timothy (1 Thess. 1:1). We will discuss many aspects of developing a team in chapter 14.

Moses' father-in-law, Jethro, advised him to share with qualified others the burdens of responsibility for the great multitude of Israelites that had left Egypt (Exod. 18). Unlike Moses, who had a large group from the beginning, most of us start off with a small group that will grow in size. When it does, the leadership must also grow in size if it is to lead effectively and meet the needs of all the people.

Becoming "Fitted Together" with Bonding Factors

Coaches work to see their players "gel" into a team. Labor unions speak of "solidarity." Something must happen for a group of unrelated individuals to become "held together" so that the Body "grows with a growth which is from God" (Col. 2:19).

Paul said to the Ephesians, "You are no longer strangers and aliens, but you are fellow citizens with the saints, and are of God's household, having been built upon the foundation of the apostles and prophets, Christ Jesus Himself being the corner stone, in whom the whole building, being fitted together is growing into a holy temple in the Lord" (Eph. 2:19-21). This "holy temple in the Lord" matures corporately as each stone is fitted into place. If the stone is properly shaped—matured—but is not in place, the temple is not complete, not mature. A singer may have a marvelous, mature voice, yet unless that singer blends and fits properly with other members of the choir, the choir will have an immature, incomplete sound. The Body of Christ matures as the individuals are properly fitted and bonded together.

Ephesians 2:14 and 4:1-13 reveal some characteristics of a group that is becoming "fitted together." These characteristics are the bonding factors that enable the Body to grow "into a holy temple in the Lord." They are (1) unity, (2) interpersonal relationships, (3) shared ministry.

Unity (oneness with the group) was first revealed as a major concern of Jesus. On the night when He was betrayed He prayed that His disciples "may all be one; even as Thou, Father, art in Me, and I in Thee" (John 17:21). Unity was a key concern for the Church. Paul said, "For He Himself is our peace, who made both groups into one . . . . being diligent to preserve the *unity* of the Spirit in the bond of peace. There is . . . *one* Lord, *one* faith, *one* baptism, *one* God and Father of all who is over all and through all and in all" (Eph. 2:14; 4:3-6, italics added; see also Phil. 1:27; 2:2). Through faith in Jesus Christ, Christians share the intrinsic unity of new life in Christ; they are literally one Body in Christ.

Unity develops in the Body: (1) as each participant grows in personal commitment to the group as a whole; (2) as each person feels he or she belongs to the group; and (3) as the group develops a positive spirit.

Unity will grow as you teach, exhort, encourage and in other ways motivate your people to understand that commitment to a church or fellowship of Christians is an expression of personal commitment to the Body of Christ. "I am committed to this group. This is where I worship and serve. This is where I am supported." Commitment is to the whole, not just a part. When a person joins a local church, he or she usually does not consciously say, "I commit myself to Bill, Jane and Jill who are my friends in this church." Commitment to the group involves commitment to the group's goals; sharing in the group's dreams and visions; supporting and participating in the group even when you disagree with something going on; regularly attending every meeting of the group, unless a higher priority in your life intervenes whether you feel like it or not, not just when it is convenient for you to go. This group is *your* group.

Unity develops when the people feel they belong to the group. The sense of belonging is sometimes called "community" and is the feeling that "my group is a family of which I am an accepted participant." It is being a part of a whole even though you may not know every person in it. You all have faith in Christ and are all one in Him. You feel cared for. You make personal friends and serve the whole in some ministry.

Many things contribute to the sense of belonging. The practice of receiving members in an official manner is one of them. The act of joining the church is more than an expression of commitment to the group; it actually increases commitment and a sense of belonging. We help people belong as we help them make friends with others in the group and as we help them find ways to serve the group in some ministry.

The spirit of a church or group contributes to unity. This spirit, this morale, is the esprit de corps of a group, the spirit of the body, and is tremendously important for the life of a fellowship. Have you ever walked into a wor-

ship service and sensed an electricity and a spirit that lifted
you and pulled you into the group? Conversely, have you
ever entered a church and discovered it was D.O.A.,
Dead On Arrival? The difference is the esprit de corps.
The spirit of a group is like the self-image of a person. A
group with a positive spirit is confident about what is happening in the group now and looks forward to the future; it
feels good about itself. It offers a positive growth environment to its members and is attractive to visitors. Spirit
carries momentum: a positive spirit builds on itself; a negative spirit is difficult to change.

To build the unity of your group, seek creative
answers to the questions: "How can we build our commitment, sense of belonging, and spirit (CBS)? What will
increase our people's commitment to our church (group,
fellowship)? What will enable our people to feel they
belong to our group? What will build the spirit of our
group?"

The second bonding factor of a group that enables people to be fitted together is *interpersonal relationships*. This
term describes that which links together the parts, or individual members, of the Body of Christ. Where unity is
oneness with the group, interpersonal relationships means
oneness with individuals. This is crucial. The better people know one another and know about one another, the
closer they fit into the group and the stronger the group
will become. This comes from Ephesians 4:16: "The
whole body, being fitted and held together by that which
every joint supplies."

Two fascinating Greek words—*haphé* and [*sundesmos*], are variously translated as ligament, bond, or joint.
They refer to the connective tissue that joins parts of the
body together. Paul uses *haphe* in Ephesians 4:16 and *sun-*

desmos in Colossians 2:19: "The entire body, being supplied and held together by the joints and ligaments [*sundesmos*], grows with a growth which is from God." These bonds are personal relationships: "knit together in love" (Col. 2:2) and "put on love, which is the perfect bond of unity" (3:14), to know a love that bonds person to person; "unity of the Spirit in the bond of peace" (Eph. 4:3), the peace between God and people and between people and people, which has been made possible by Christ's death on the cross (see Eph. 2:14-16). The basis of Christian relationships and unity is the peace and love initiated by God and shared between people (see Eph. 2:1-7).

Person-to-person relationships—two people growing in commitment to each other, trust in each other, service to each other, love for each other and for Jesus Christ—are at the heart of fellowship. As we grow in deep relationships with an increasing number of people we create a web of relationships.[1]

A growing web of relationships ties you to the group with ever-strengthening bonds. As Ecclesiastes says, "A cord of three strands is not quickly torn apart" (4:12). We want to help every person's own web of relationships to grow and strengthen. We want to develop a web that connects all the people in our group together in personal friendships so that each person senses a growing security and has as special place within the group. In a network no one person can be the key to the group's health and growth as a whole.

Shared meals, Small Group meetings, and prayer partners encourage webbing. Avoid a purely program view of ministry: a speaker and dessert. Rather than chatting for 15 minutes over dessert then spending 45 minutes (or more) listening to a speaker, have a dinner where people sit eight to a table, getting to know one another. After din-

ner they could move away from the tables for a brief program of 10 to 15 minutes, then join a different group of
eight people for dessert for another good period of friendship building.

Small-Group Bible studies of seven to twelve people,
meeting in homes, is another way for people to get to
know each other in new ways. Section IV offers a more in-
depth look at small groups.

To avoid the negative aspects of webbing—forming
cliques that become a barrier to growth, small groups
should encourage their members to focus on people who
are not in their groups. The motto is "Ministry in public—
friendship in private." In a public setting such as Sunday
worship services, the members of the group talk to non-
group members, of course, not only to each other. Con-
versations among members may best occur when the
group meets or when members are in contact with each
other in private settings.

It is normal for us to want to deepen old friendships
because it strengthens our position in a group. Also, positions of influence and leadership usually rise from an existing network. But if the group fences out new people, it will
eventually stagnate for lack of new relationships and
broadening friendships.

The third bonding factor of a group is that of *a shared
ministry*. The Body of Christ is not simply an organization,
it is a living organism, a body, consisting of mutually
dependent parts. A group matures just as a body matures,
with member parts operating properly according to their
particular gifts, "We are to grow up . . . according to the
proper working of each individual part" (Eph. 4:15-16).
The bonding factor of shared ministry means that every
person in the group must be actively building other people

and using gifts in service. Ministry is not a job reserved for the minister or other leaders. It is the responsibility and privilege of every member of the group.

We build ministry in a group, first, as we develop the Send-Them concept in people. They must believe, "I am sent to serve, sent to minister to the people in my world." Second, we help people learn to build up a few other people using the principles described in chapters 4 and 5. Third, we build ministry in a group as we enable the people to use their spiritual gifts in the group. Peter said, "As each one has received a special gift, employ it in serving one another (1 Pet. 4:10). Some can teach, some serve, some exhort, others heal (see Matt. 25:14-30; Rom. 12; 1 Cor. 12; Eph. 4).

If everyone in a group is to have a place to serve, leaders must plan ahead. I recall a college student, trained in youth work, who asked her pastor how she could serve the church during the summer. He literally couldn't think of a place to use her! He had not planned ahead so that there were enough places for service opportunities. Finding a place of service that "fits" everyone may take some experimenting. Some find their niches right away and are challenged for a lifetime; others may cycle from one service to another for years before their best opportunity for ministry is clear.

We do want people to find their niches and use their gifts; but the emphasis is on *serving*, not just finding their gifts so they can be fulfilled. Sometimes the church or group may need us to work in a capacity that does not necessarily fit within the framework of our spiritual gifts. No matter, as servants we give of ourselves according to the need of our fellowship. Sometimes, God develops a new spiritual gift in us by this method. This is often true if a person changes churches or moves to a new town and

finds a new church. The spiritual gift he or she used at the
old fellowship may not be needed the same way in the
new. The whole purpose of spiritual gifts is for the "building up of the body of Christ" in the local church as well as
the universal Body of Christ (Eph. 4:12).

When each person has a place to belong, someone to
love and something to do, he fits! He finds great satisfac-
tion in a life shared with others as the bonding factors bind
them to the fellowship. He can then say, "I am committed
to and belong to this group (unity). I have friends to love
(relationships). I have a place to serve (ministry)."

Encouraging "Nesting"

Frequently, Congregations have smaller groups within
them—couples' ministry, men's group, youth group, singles' group, small-group Bible studies. I refer to these
sub-groups as a nested structure because they nest within
each other (see fig. 1). Each sub-group operates with a dis-
tinct identity and life-style all its own as it nests within the
larger group. These groups may be roughly defined by
size: a Small Group consisting of 12 or less; a Discipleship
Community from 12-15 to 200-250; and the large group,
the Congregation, encompasses the Community and all
sub-groups and individuals (see fig. 2). C. Peter Wagner
describes these groups as the cell, the congregation, and
the celebration.[2] Other terms for these three groups are
cell, community, congregation[3]; person, small group,
mass. Chuck Miller calls these the spectrum of ministry.[4]

Each level in the spectrum of ministry offers us opportunity to build people. In this book we discuss four ministry patterns to build people: Person-to-Person, through
the Small Group, through the Discipleship Community,
and through the Congregation. An effective leader seeks

Nested Groups

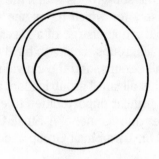

Figure 1

Nested Groups within a Church

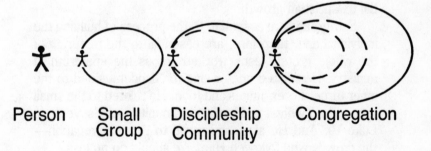

Person   Small   Discipleship   Congregation
          Group   Community

Figure 2

to build all of the sub-groups within the portion of the spectrum of ministry for which he or she is responsible. For example, a person in charge of a Discipleship Community which has small groups, seeks to build the whole Community, the Small Groups, and the individuals within it. He or she insures that all small group leaders are trained and that they receive regular opportunities to express their needs and receive encouragement. A Small Group leader would seek to build his own Small Group and each person within it.

Each group size enables Christian growth in a unique way because each size offers different experiences and opportunities. In a Small Group there are more intense relationships, more opportunities to speak, and better intimacy and accountability. Bonding factors become stronger. A church or fellowship with many Small groups increases growth opportunities for its people. On the other hand, a larger group generates a greater sense of celebration and openness to new people and offers greater resources to help people in need. Both groups are essential to Christian growth.

Sub-groups are essential; to the process of building the individual and, therefore, are essential to the maturing of the whole group. Jesus worked across the spectrum of ministry. He related one-on-one to Nicodemus and to the inner three, Peter, James and John. He related to the small group, the Twelve, and to the community—the seventy in Luke 10. And He also ministered to the congregation—the crowds who followed Him. We should do no less.

Growing in the Image of Christ as a Group

A group grows in the image of Christ just as an individual does, except it matures *as a group*. "And they were con-

tinually devoting themselves to the apostles' teaching and
to fellowship, to the breaking of bread and to prayer"
(Acts 2:42), is how Luke described the Jerusalem Church.

Just as the growth of the individual involves the three
dimensions of the new life, the new mind, and the new life-
style, so does the growth of the group. The church as a
whole is in God and receives its new life from Him. In
assessing the new life of the group we would ask: "Do the
people know Christ? Do we need to share the gospel with
any or all of our people?"

The new mind (knowledge and thought) of the group
develops as its members and leaders, first, share a knowledge of Scripture and a common theology, and, second,
think together concerning the life which God has given
them. "Now I exhort you, brethren, by the name of our
Lord Jesus Christ, that you all agree, and there be no divisions among you, but you be made complete in the *same
mind* and in the same judgment" (1 Cor. 1:10, italics
added). As a group expresses its own understanding of
Scripture, the resulting confession of faith or doctrine
becomes its basic expression of corporate knowledge.
Then, as each member of the group matures in depth and
breadth of Christian knowledge, the group as a whole
matures. "Is every person learning? Do we clearly and
consistently teach the basic doctrines of Christianity?"

A corporate Body of Christians also shares in the new
life-style as a group. The Hebrew prophets continually
challenged God's people with truth and their failure as a
people to live the truth. Paul said to the Philippian church,
"Make my joy complete by being of the same mind, maintaining the same love, united in spirit, intent on one purpose" (Phil. 2:2).

The group thus grows as a unit in the Three Life-Style
Relationships of Jesus Christ (the Triune God, the Body of

Christ, the people in the world). The people together practice the same basic life-style marks as the individual does. These Eleven Life-Style Marks would be grouped together for the Body as a whole in the four major functions of the church and its people. For example, renewal, worship, prayer are all expressed in *Worship*; word is expressed in *Instruction*; family, fellowship, stewardship, and ministry fall under *Fellowship*; and compassion, evangelism and work find their activity in *Expression*. These observances of the Life-Style Marks in a group can easily be remembered by the acrostic WIFE.

To assess your group's Christian life-style, ask, "How effective are Worship, Instruction, Fellowship, and Expression in our group?" A church that is growing in maturity would be able to say, "We are a worship center, a teaching center, a fellowship center, and an expression or outreach center." Enabling the development of each corporate discipline builds the group in balance.

We, of course, are aware that we will never reach perfect maturity in the group any more than we can reach perfection as individuals. There are inhibitors to group maturity just as the "old self" inhibits the growth of the individual. Jesus was aware of this. He spoke repeatedly in His kingdom parables about wheat and tares, good fish and foul fish, sheep and goats (see Matt. 13). His picture is of the Church as it is in this life. The Body of Christ, represented by wheat, good fish, and sheep in the parables, is mixed with the tares, foul fish, and goats. Separation will not occur until the consummation and judgment (Matt. 25:40-44). This does not mean we exclude those whom we discern are not yet wheat, good fish, or sheep, because in doing so we deny people outside the faith the opportunity to associate with Christians and to be encouraged to meet Christ. The point is that the spectrum of

Christian maturity in any church is broad—from non-Christian to committed disciple. The church will always have room to grow! I see three areas of inhibitors to maturity as a group.

First, there are "outsiders" inside the church. These are the people who need our witness and our ministry until they surrender their wills to the will of God in Jesus Christ. Second, there are "insiders," Christians in the church, who choose to live according to the influence of the "old self." The apostle Paul warned the elders of a church he loved dearly, that "from among your own selves men will arise, speaking perverse things, to draw away the disciples after them" (Acts 20:30). Unfortunately, every church has its share of jealousies, divisions and resentments among the "insiders."

A third area that sometimes inhibits growth of the fellowship as a whole is division among the key leadership of the church; remember that Jesus had Judas!

Should these inhibitors deter us from striving toward perfection as a group? No! We offer leadership; we make peace where possible; we trust God to bless the results of our efforts.

Assessing the Group

We work at developing capable leaders, becoming fitted together, encouraging "nesting," and growing in Christian life-style to reach the end of ministry—growing in the image of Christ. How do we assess our group, whether it numbers seven or seventy, whether it is a church, a large fellowship, a small group or a family, to evaluate how we are doing? Look at the way we started this chapter by describing how an orchestra illustrates the Body of Christ.

Leadership: Are we practicing the double focus of ministry, (1) on the individual and (2) on the church, by using a planning process?

Bonding factors: Is there a commitment to the group so that the individual members are able to sense belonging: "This is my group" (unity)? Is there a strong esprit de corps, or group morale (unity)? Is there a growing web of relationships (relationships)? Are there broken relationships that need to be mended (relationships)? Do people love one another in practice (ministry)? Has every member found his or her place of personal ministry (ministry)?

Nested groups: Are there nested groups with a growing number of sub-groups?

Knowledge and life-style: Are we growing in effectiveness in worship, instruction, fellowship, and expression?

The very life-style of the fellowship offers the major source of group building principles. For example, worship is not only a mark of corporate life-style, it is also a means by which the unity of the fellowship grows. Worship, Prayer, Teaching, Family Life, Fellowship, Stewardship, Ministry, Leadership, Compassion, Evangelism are life-style marks of the Body of Christ that also build the Body of Christ as they are lived. Thus, the life-style marks of the group are both *ends and means* of Christian life-style. They are both the ends of ministry and the principles of ministry! When leaders encourage and enable the group to practice Christian life-style, that very life-style will build the group in Christ.

Tying it all Together is discussed in the next chapter.

CHAPTER 7

Tying It All Together: The Unity of Ministry

Do you ever feel that your ministry is fragmented with counseling, preparation, teaching, worship leading, and administration? How do you bring the parts into a unified whole? One afternoon I was studying a blackboard on which I had written the master principles of building people: Prayer, Care, With-Me, Word and Send-Them, as well as the Four Major Functions of the church and its people: Worship, Instruction, Fellowship and Expression (WIFE). In an "Aha" moment, I suddenly realized that the principles of building people and the marks of group life-style were one and the same.

Group Life-Style Functions	Principles of Building People
Worship	Prayer
Instruction	Word
Fellowship	With-Me
	Care
Expression	Send-Them

This revelation was tremendously significant to me as I thought about the double focus of ministry: building people and building the group into the image of Christ. This chapter is about how to unify your ministry of building the individual and the Body. All ministry to the Body builds the Body, whether the primary focus is on the individual or on the group. Unity of ministry means that when you build the person you also build his or her group; and when you build a group you also build each person in that group. Discipleship and fellowship enable each other. Person building and group building are Body building ministries.

To begin with, who is responsible for building the Body? Who initiates it?

The individual can initiate Body building as he or she senses the need of a person or group and begins to practice the principles of ministry in his or her personal *lifestyle*. The group can initiate Body building as its leadership creates *program* to meet the needs of the group. Thus both the individual and the group (by means of its leadership) may exercise the double focus of ministry.

Your Double Focus of Ministry

Every person can have a double focus in his or her ministry. It doesn't have to be one or the other. You may say, "I am seeking to build John and Janet Fry, Bill and Mary

Green, Joe Brady, and Margaret Evans. I am going to do this by applying to a few the principles of building individuals. I am also going to build my fellowship as I serve as elder, deacon, usher, Sunday School teacher or musician." You have now determined that you are going to have a double focus of ministry—to the individual, and to the group.

If you are a member of a congregation your double focus of ministry is done through the exercise of your gifts, spiritual and natural. If you are the pastor or other professional leader within the congregation your double focus of ministry is done through your leadership. Thus, every Christian can share ministry as Christ intended we should. Just how do you go about beginning your double focus of ministry?

Find your few. We have already talked about Jesus and how He ministered to a few. Your few should, first, be people you can challenge to grow in Christ along with you. Pray regularly, "Lord, who do you want me to focus on?" As you do you will find you are drawn to certain people whom you sense you can invite to grow in discipleship with you. Today, my few includes three individual men, the people in a Wednesday evening couple's Bible study, and the people on a ministry team.

Then next, not only do you feel drawn to a few, there will be a few who are drawn to grow in Christ with you. These people can be with you when you offer opportunity such a Discipleship Community (chap. 12) in which anyone who wants to be "With Me" can do so. Of course, those "few" can be only three or as many as eighty, depending on the size of the wider Congregation, yet they will be those who step forward indicating an extra interest in growing in Christ with you.

Your "few" could be just your family; however, if we all did only this, the Body of Christ would be limited in size as well as in depth of spirituality. We also have to focus on a few other adults in addition to our own families. No matter where you are spiritually at this moment, there is someone else you can encourage in Christ.

One time a man approached me and said, "Stan, I want to grow in my spiritual life. Will you meet with me?"

I answered, "Rob, it would be a privilege to grow in Christ along with you. When I visit the hospitals on Friday afternoon, will you join me?" Rob agreed and for months we watched God work in life and death situations in hospitals; then we met together for a time of conversation and prayer. We memorized two Bible verses each week as a means of studying Scripture together. Our time was tremendously fruitful in both our lives.

You cannot personally build everyone in your fellowship because of the time factor. It takes in-depth involvement to build this quality of relationships. Occasionally, someone approaches me about my being his or her spiritual director when I simply do not have time for another person. I try to refer that person to someone else who will offer the needed direction.

The pastor of a church of 200 told me that preaching twice a week and other pastoral duties left him "too busy to build a few disciples." Yet, he said it with sadness. The pressures of administering program, preaching or teaching, and pastoring can dominate a pastor's life and schedule, leaving him no time to focus on a few.

If we are to take seriously Jesus' model for building people we need to adjust the traditional approach to ministry—which is usually preaching and administering the sacraments to the crowds, focusing on the individual only during times of distress. We need to do as Jesus did.

He consistently taught the many and offered pastoral care to individuals in need; but at the same time He built His few. Studying His model leads to three essential premises that allow the church to develop those who are significant spiritual leaders.

First, if you are a pastor or other leader in your church, you must *focus on a few no matter how many your "many" may be.* Whether your church has 200 or 2,000 members, you cannot focus personally on all of them. You can focus on a few with whom you can develop a deeper friendship and grow in Christ. Every pastor has discovered a few in his or her congregation who want a deeper experience with Christ. These are the few upon whom you can focus ministry. Eventually you can send them to focus on others.

Since schedule is always a problem to a church leader, you need to make building a few a matter of priority. Once you make a heart commitment to build a few, other pressures and demands of ministry will rearrange themselves around that priority.

Second, *you cannot neglect the many while you focus on the few.* Excellence in preaching, program, and pastoral care are not options. Your life must touch far more lives than the few you seek to build more deeply. A large number of people in your congregation will sense your personal interest and support as you teach, preach, visit, counsel, participate in committee work, and answer never-ending phone calls. The lay leaders in your church, your elders, deacons and other workers, who are also involved with you in growing the Body, must know that you support them in their ministry. This calls for regular contact.

Since ministry demands in a group seem to be infinite, how do you determine how much ministry is enough? I tend to think in terms of the "appropriate" level of ministry to the many. There will always be those who need or want more attention than they receive. There will always be programs that need more administrative attention than I can give. I schedule time with a few, usually in a small-group setting; then I work out my time to minister appropriately with the many.

People who were always with Jesus were at various levels of intimacy with Him. Those who were in the large groups certainly were able to receive something from Him as they listened to His teaching and witnessed His healing and received food from Him. The Twelve related to Jesus both in the large group and in more private and alone times. Thus, the Twelve received a much higher content than the masses did. Person building has its greatest impact on the few on whom you focus, but anyone who is around you, even in large groups, can learn from you.

The third premise is that we must *minister to the many with the few*. This is also a way that Jesus, the Master builder of people, ministered. The Twelve did not sit at His feet only; they were equipped to minister and sent to minister. Jesus equipped and motivated them to build others in Christ. When He ministered to large crowds, the Twelve were with Him. Jesus ministered to the Twelve, then He ministered with the Twelve in the lives of those in the larger group. If you are a Sunday School teacher, ask your few to assist you. If you are an usher, ask them to usher with you. If you are an administrator, ask them to administer with you. The goal is not to get them to do your work; it is to allow them to experience ministry *with* you.

As a Small-Group leader you should ask two or three

people to assist you in caring for the group, an informal "caring hub," such as Peter, James, and John were with Jesus. These two or three learn with you how to love people and how to trust God to build other people.

There is one caution concerning ministering to a few, and that is *avoid favoritism*. If you are in a position of leadership in your church you have probably already discovered that being consistently attentive to a select few can cause other persons in the congregation to become jealous. Some people may choose to resent the attention others are receiving no matter what you do. Nevertheless, there are some useful tactics you can use to minimize this concern.

First, avoid making any public statements about your "few." I don't even say I have a few! That is like saying, "I heard a great joke today, but I'm not telling you." People may feel left out and resentful. In some cases I do not even let a person in my few know that I am focusing on him. I do not need praise or credit for serving people and for asking God to use me in their lives as I offer them a little more of myself.

Second, do not focus on your few in a public setting. In this way you avoid becoming a clique. Use the motto, "Ministry in public—friendship in private." In a public setting, such as Sunday morning, you and your few disperse to minister to other individuals among the many, or together you minister to the many. You do not talk just to each other. You know you will see each other at other times for personal interaction.

Third, give the whole congregation plenty of opportunity to be with you at a more personal level. I frequently ask the whole congregation to "come be with me." People who want to get near me can do so at seminars, Bible classes, men's fellowships, and so forth. People can get near me if they want to and I want to focus on the person who steps forward and says, "I'm interested in walking on 'higher ground,' as the old hymn says."

We do not focus on the few so that we can assert spiritual superiority; rather we do it to serve them and teach them to serve others. I would never go to my few and say, "I have the truth. You don't have the truth. Sit down. I'm going to give you the truth." That's an insult. Even though I may have more knowledge and understanding in some areas of my life than another does, I also benefit and grow toward maturity by what others share with me. My approach is, "Let's discover together what the Scripture says. Let's discover Christ together and both of us will grow in Him (see Rom. 1:11-12). I know I have learned some things that I must share. I also know that I have much more to learn. Building people is always a mutual experience; you grow and I grow as we are together" (see Prov. 27:17).

Throughout this book I outline four patterns which you may use to build those "few" who are interested in growth (Person-to-Person Ministry; Starting a Small Group; Nurturing a Small Group Movement; Organizing the Discipleship Community). These are meant to be patterns. You will need to alter them to fit your church. By assessing your own situation and the needs of the people whom God has given you to build, you will find the pattern that suits you best.

Find Your Function in the Body

Paul told the Romans that "God has allotted to each a measure of faith. For just as we have many members in one body and all the members do not have the same function, so we, who are many, are one body in Christ, and individually members one of another. And since we have gifts that differ according to the grace given to us, let each exercise them accordingly" (12:3-6). In other words, "Find your gift and use it in the Body to build well-being and maturity to individuals and to the Body as a whole."

When you direct your spiritual gifts, personality and unique life experiences towards serving the Body, you will find your special place in the Body and will begin to mature towards the image of Christ. No matter what your gift(s) is—teaching, administering, leading, serving, exhorting, sharing Christ, compassion (C. Peter Wagner lists 27 spiritual gifts)—you must serve! Some ministries are public and very visible; others are private and "invisible." For example, a pastor, elder, deacon, teacher, church officer, usher, or musician offers visible service to their local Body. They receive a lot of affirmation and gratitude (and their share of criticism as well). Many others serve without public recognition, without an "official" job or title. Your service may be to set up chairs or get refreshments or offer rides to church or to other activities. When someone asks, "Where do you serve?" you say very legitimately, "I serve my group by helping where I see a need." You see, it is not important whether your role is visible or invisible. What is important is that you have a place to serve and that you and God both know about it, and that you are consciously, regularly doing it to build the group of which you are a part.

Pray that God will (1) give you "a few" that you might build; also (2) that you would find your place of service within your church or fellowship. It may take you six months or six years to find that place. Yet, when you discover where to use your gifts you may use them to build your group for the rest of your life.

When people in your church begin to focus on a few

and to find their place of service, God will then work through them to build your local Body—His church—in the image of His Son.

In the next chapter we will talk about how to establish a deliberate yet simple planning process for the double focus of ministry.

NOTE: Portions of chapter 7 appeared in "Leadership Journal," Volume 8, Number 3, Summer 1987. Used by permission.

CHAPTER 8

Implementing a Plan

Whether or not we are aware of it, we all live by planning our time. We say, "Tomorrow I have to go to the grocery store." That's planning. Or, "Johnny wants to go to Harvard when he finishes high school." More planning. We plan families, budgets, vacations; we plan for careers; we plan to plan.

Scripture is filled with examples of people who made plans. Joseph planned how to store grain to feed the Egyptians and his own family during the famine. Joshua had a plan to conquer Jericho. Jesus operated according to a plan: "My time is not yet at hand." Paul planned to visit Rome. In each case, God gave and/or directed the developing of the plan and the results. "The mind of man plans his way, but the Lord directs his steps" (Prov. 16.9).

It takes a planning process to build an equipping ministry. It will not happen unless you plan for it to happen. When we plan, we do it in one of two ways: intentionally or intuitionally. We plan intentionally when, individually or with a leadership team, we evaluate "Where do we want to go?" and "How are we going to get there?" It is leadership by objective as we determine what objectives we want to reach with our people.

On the other hand, the intuitional planner plans by a "feel" of what a person or group needs. It is leadership by opportunity as intuitional planning is often spontaneous, responding to a need in the group or new ministry opportunity. Such a planner acts out of an innate gift and/or prior training. Like intentional planning, intuitional planning results in following specific steps to action. The danger of intuitional planning for a group is that leaders tend to plan only toward their "favorite" goals and emphases.

A leader who is schooled and experienced can become very effective in both intentional and intuitive planning. Such a person has a "trained" intuition that senses a change in the needs of people. He or she also is capable of intentional planning that addresses a need systematically.

The Intentional Planning Process

In recent years we have heard a lot about managing by objectives. This process highlights the key steps in any effective planning process: goals, plan of action, budgeting, organization, and evaluation. The advantage of such a structured intentional planning process is that it ensures (1) clear goals, (2) clear programs to reach the goals, and (3) clear accountability as to who is responsible to reach them. The disadvantages are (1) the possibility of overplanning (developing so many goals and programs that the group cannot achieve them all), (2) underplanning by jumping to solutions and skipping important planning steps.

Congregations, programs, Discipleship Communities and Small Groups respond positively to a regular intentional planning process that leads toward well-being and maturity. The planning process should also be simple enough to allow the more intuitive person to plan effectively without being frustrated by the process. Such planning includes three steps.

The first step is the process of *needs assessment*, prayerful discernment of where the group needs to grow in light of the purpose of ministry—the well-being and Christian discipleship of the people. The second step is to review relevant *principles of ministry*. Third, is *program planning:* developing goals and a plan of action designed to meet needs and use principles. These three steps, of course, are the three ingredients of ministry: People, Principles, and Practice which we have spoken of throughout the book.

Step 1: Needs assessment. In needs assessment you evaluate where you are in light of where you are going. And in our double focus of ministry we focus on the needs of each person in the group and the needs of the group as a whole. A need is the gap between where the person presently is and where he or she might grow in well-being and discipleship. To begin assessing the individual you need to pray about each person in the group, asking God, *"Is it well with this person?";* "How can we build this person in Christ?" In order to enable well-being you may ask, "How is John physically, emotionally, and socially? Does he need shelter, a better self-esteem, help in relationships, a job? Is he going through a time of pain, grief, anxiety or insecurity?"

To assess John's level of discipleship, you should ask

God, *"Is John growing in discipleship?* Is there growth in the new life through faith in Jesus Christ and the filling of the Holy Spirit? Is he growing in new mind by learning and understanding Scripture? Is he growing in Christian life-style?"

Additional guides to assessing the extent of his growth include the *Three Relationships*—the Triune God (the Great Commandment), the Body of Christ (the New Commandment), the work of Christ in the world (the Great Commission); and the *Seven Spiritual Disciplines*—renewal, Word and prayer, family strength, fellowship with Christians, stewardship of money, ministry to others, and work. (See the Content Chart (Appendix A) for a detailed overview of life-style material.

To assess the well-being and maturity of the group as a whole, reflect on the group's practice of the major *Life-Style Marks*—"Are we growing in effectiveness in Worship, Instruction, Fellowship, Expression?

When we assess needs of a group we seek to be aware of *problems* that represent some difficulty with an aspect of the well-being of the group, and *possibilities* which are underdeveloped arenas of ministry. For example, a person planning for a group of high school student might write:

Group Life-Style   Needs

Worship   Our students need to learn that music is a means of wor-ship, not an end in itself (a problem).

Instruction   A method of inductive Bible study would help the stu-dents in their quiet time (a possibility).

Fellowship   Many new people have come recently but are having trouble entering the group's web of relationships (a problem).

Expression   A "How to Share Your Faith" seminar would really help the students turn outward (a possibility).

Step 2: Principles of Ministry. The second step of effective ministry planning is usually skipped. In this step we review: The *People-Building Principles*—Prayer, care, With-Me, Word, Send-Them, Teaching, Shared Meals, Fun, Retreats, Challenge and Motivation (see Chap. 4 for additional principles).

Group-Building Principles (chap. 6) include: *Leadership:* "Are we practicing the double focus of ministry and using a regular planning process?" *Bonding Factors:* Unity—"Is there a commitment to the group and a sense of belonging? Is there a strong group morale?"; Relationships—"Is there a growing network of relationships? Are there broken relationsihps being mended?"; Ministry—"Are they loving one another in practice? Does every member have a personal ministry?" *Nested Groups:* "Are there nested groups with a growing number of subgroups?—Small Groups and Discipleship Communities within the congregation?"

Ministry is not the mechanical combination of needs and principles. Rather, as you discern needs and review principles you can devise programs that utilize the means of ministry to reach the ends of ministry.

Step 3: Program Planning. In this step you need to set measurable, achievable goals and devise a program or plan of action to meet the needs by solving problems and realizing possibilities. When planning, most people can think of more needs than the group can ever begin to address. Thus the leadership must determine which needs are priority. Most groups, whether a Congregation or a program, can only deal with a few new ministry initiatives or emphases at any given time.

It is possible to avoid overplanning at this step if the planner selects only high priority needs and begins to design ministry initiatives, or programs, that deal with more than one need at once.

Suppose, for example, you were planning to begin a ministry to single adults. In Step 1, Needs Assessment, you and others developing this ministry with you might list the following on a chalkboard:

> The need for emotional support
> The need for fun
> The need for self-esteem
> The need for spiritual growth
> The need for friends
> The need to belong.

Reflecting on these needs might lead you to the following statement of goals:

> Goal 1: To offer opportunity for spiritual growth, friendship, and emotional support to single adults
>
> Goal 2: To offer an enjoyable place to belong for single adults
>
> Goal 3: To offer emotional support to those experiencing the pain of divorce
>
> Goal 4: To develop friendship among single adults.

Then in planning Step 2 you would write down relevant principles of ministry:

Nested structure—both large-number and Small-Group experience

A balance of Word-Share-Prayer (Discipleship Triangle)

WIFE—Worship, Instruction, Fellowship, Expression

Bonding Factors—Unity, Relationships, Ministry to one another.

Finally, after reflecting on these goals and the principles of ministry, the planning team can propose the following tentative program:

Tuesday, 7:30 P.M.—Large Group. An upbeat time of song, skits and teaching
8:15 P.M.—Small Groups to practice Word, Share, Prayer together.
Friday, twice a month—Socials in homes (fellowship and expression-outreach)
Sunday, 9:30 A.M.—Sunday Schools for instruction
11:00 A.M.—Worship
Every day—Encourage members to phone each other daily.

How detailed actual planning becomes depends on how familiar the leaders are with needs and principles and the amount of time they have to plan. Even novice leaders, however, can quickly participate in a planning effort more detailed than this illustration.

Planning for the Congregation

Before you can plan for the life of your congregation, you need a clear, concise statement expressing your church's major aims. Such a statement will guide the program of the Congregation and can be grasped by the majority of the members. For example, one such statement reads:

> The purpose of the Pleasant Hills Community Presbyterian Church as a Congregation and as Christians is to grow in our commitment to the Triune God, to the Body of Christ, and to the Work of Christ in the World.

A church with a goal of mission might have a statement that reads:

> Our purpose as a congregation and as Christians is to grow in our knowledge and worship of the Triune God, to build the well-being and maturity of the Body of Christ, and to serve the people in the world on behalf of Jesus Christ.

Within this statement is enclosed The Three Life-Style Relationships: the Triune God, the Body of Christ, and the World. This statement guides you as to how you can begin assessing your congregation so that you can receive direction for your planning process. For example:

Triune God	Worship	Worship
		Prayer
	Instruction	Teaching
The Body	Fellowship	Family
of Christ		Fellowship
		Stewardship

		Leadership
		Compassion (in the church)
Work of Christ in the World	Expression	Compassion (outside the church)
		Evangelism

How detailed your planning becomes depends on how much time your leaders have and how well trained they are. You may use the basic Four Group Life-Style Functions—Worship, Instruction, Fellowship, and Expression (WIFE), asking basic questions along the line of those found earlier in this chapter. If your congregation or ministry needs a more detailed planning, you can adapt and expand the list of life-style marks. You must organize and plan around these areas if you are to accomplish your church's aim. For example:

Life-Style Marks	Committee
Worship	Worship Committee
Prayer	Worship Committee
Word	Christian Education Committee
Family	Christian Education Committee
Fellowship	Discipleship/Fellowship Groups
Stewardship	Stewardship Committee
Leadership	Staff, Elders and Trustees
Compassion	Deacons
Evangelism	Evangelism Committee

Using the Three-Step Planning Process—(1) Needs

Assessment, (2) Principles of Ministry, (3) Program Planning—each committee or the leadership team assesses the needs in each Life-Style Mark for which they are responsible, reviews the principles of ministry, and determines goals and action steps needed to reach them.

You may need a more detailed planning process than just three steps for church-wide planning and long-range goal setting:

1. Needs assessment, by Life-Style Marks
2. Review of Principles of Ministry
3. Goal setting
4. Program (proposals to reach goals)
5. Personnel (accountability)
6. Budgeting
7. Evaluation.

The Reason for Planning

You do whatever it takes to make your church or ministry aware of the double focus of ministry—"How can we build each person in the image of Christ?" which considers the well-being and Christian discipleship of each person, and "How can we build our group in the image of Christ?" which has to do with bonding and the life of the fellowship. Both discipleship and fellowship, spiritual formation and group formation, are essential to building the Body of Christ.

If you do not approach your ministry with these assessment questions, your fellowship runs the risk of falling into the programmed routine of worship services, pot lucks, speakers, and youth activities, without any real growth in the personal discipleship of the people and the factors that bond them together. Ministry then becomes solely the administration of programs and the offering of care in crises.

It is important to understand that *the maturity of a group is independent of any given program*. The same group of people may attend a church together over a lifetime. Events will come, change, and go. The maturity of the group is not reflected in the number or nature of their programs per se, but in the growing discipleship of the people and in the maturity of the fellowship—the leadership, the bonding factors, the nested structure, and the life-style which these programs enable among the people over the lifetime of the group.

For example, a group may begin an evening with an existing network of relationships. Each person who comes fits somewhere inside or outside of the network. If the program ends, and people have not developed new relationships or sustained and deepened the relationship they already had, the program has failed from the perspective of developing a growing, maturing web of friendship.

Try stepping back from your group's programs and ask, "Are people really growing in Christ?" Are we really strengthening the bonding factors? Are we really expressing the corporate Christian life-style (WIFE)?" If not, then it is time to design programs that will effectively build your people in discipleship and enable the group to grow in Bonding Factors and Worship, Instruction, Fellowship and Expression.

An event is a valid ministry when it fulfills the goal of moving toward well-being and maturity. It is not uncommon for program to become an end in itself. Sometimes, leaders or committees will initiate events more to justify their own existence than to move toward a stated goal. If the person-centered ministry question—"How can we build each person in the image of Christ?"—is not answered before an event is planned, that event will be activity for "people without faces," not true ministry. In other words, the leaders will be so concerned with the details of administering the event (securing a speaker, getting the refreshments, arranging a location, and other such details) that attention to the needs of each person of the group by name and how the program will build each person is often overlooked. Regularly assessing your events will insure that each program is geared toward helping your people—and your group as a whole—to grow in the image of Christ.

Program should be the last step in planning ministry. We begin with the needs of our people and our group; then we review basic principles of ministry, such as Prayer, Care, Word, the spectrum of ministry (nested groups), and Bonding Factors. Then we begin to initiate programs that meet those needs.

The intentional planning process begins with a systematic review of the needs of the people as individuals and with the group as a whole. The next step is to set goals and plan programs to reach those goals. Intuitive planning, because it responds to changing needs and opportunities, helps leaders adjust the program to meet the changing needs. Both types of planning done regularly, will lead people toward growing in the image of Christ.

Plans are never set in concrete. They should change as needs change. Planning is a tool, not a result, of leadership.

SECTION IV

THE PRACTICE OF
PEOPLE-BUILDING MINISTRY

9. Starting a Small Group
Getting it off the Ground
Designing a Program to Fit the Group
Choosing Small Group Commitments

10. Leading the Small Group
The Role of a Leader
A Guide for the Meetings
Small Group Commitments
More Help for the Leader

11. Nurturing a Small Group Movement
The "Control Center"
Making More Small Groups

12. Forming the Discipleship Community
Organizing from Scratch
Reorganizing an Existing Community
Planning the Program

13. Developing a Ministry Team
What Kind of Person Should Be on the Ministry
Team?
How Is a Ministry Team Developed?
What Makes Up a Typical Ministry Team Meeting?

14. Building the Congregation
How to Begin
Choosing a People-Building Pattern
Some Practical Examples
Assess, Plan, and Act

15. Getting Started

CHAPTER 9

Starting a Small Group

When my wife, Ann Marie, and I determined to start one of our first Small Groups, we spent nearly four months praying about the people we would ask to meet with us. We finally asked four other couples to join us.

Our group met each Thursday night to study the Bible (no one "taught a lesson"), share personal lives and events, and to pray conversationally. We made some basic commitments to one another. For example, we made a commitment that we would attend every group meeting for the initial six weeks (or whatever time period you choose); we made a commitment to confidentiality, nothing that was said in the group would ever be repeated to persons outside the group; we made a commitment that we would spend one hour of preparation in personal Bible study each week.

In the course of our time together we experienced many of life's joys and trials. One family had their first pregnancy; another faced surgery for a child; another dealt with the loss of their business. As we supported one another and grew in our personal disciplines of prayer and Bible study, we discovered the two major strengths of the Small Group. It is (1) a caring fellowship that offers support in time of need and (2) a discipleship group that encourages one another to grow in our walk with Christ.

The Small Group is the basic group size of the Body of Christ. It is the building block of all other ministry groups and is essential for developing active disciples. In the intimacy and accountability of the small group you can be fully known and supported; you can share the joys, as well as the deep personal struggles, knowing that you will be supported and that your confidence will be kept. The Small Group is the key group for building people.

You may choose, through prayer and reflection, the people you want to be with you in a Small Group just as Jesus chose the Twelve from the many (see Luke 6) or, as we will discuss later, you involve those who respond to a public announcement about the Small Group. These should be people who have shown an interest in wanting to grow. In time, some of those in your Small Group may be able to start other groups. The group may number up to twelve people, small enough so that everyone can have a significant personal relationship with everyone else. Someone has defined a Small Group as the "number of people who can sit around a table." The group can be comprised of four to seven members of the same gender, three to five couples, and a mixture of couples and singles, as long as everyone feels free to share personal needs and insights with the group. Although they should feel free to remain silent, the purpose of the group is to share needs, joys, blessings and insights from God.

A Small Group needs one or two leaders who will be responsible for the overall life and direction of the group, although weekly leadership responsibilities could be passed around.

Now let us consider two aspects of building the Small Group: Getting it off the Ground and Choosing a Program to Follow. In the next chapter we will talk about the Leadership of the Small Group.

Getting It off the Ground

If it has not already been done, you should first gain approval or permission from the appropriate leadership of the church or ministry—the pastor, fellowship leader, church board, leadership committee—if your group is to be a part of a larger fellowship. Some pastors are opposed to small groups either because (1) they fear that heresy may creep into the Bible study or (2) they feel the small group may become a clique or (3) they once had a bad group experience personally or (4) they fear they will lose control. After watching hundreds of Small Groups, and being in many myself, I have found these problems occur very rarely. Instead, the Small Group gives the privilege of ministry to the membership as people in the Congregation learn to build one another in their groups.

I know of one pastor who feared heresy so much that he insisted on being present at every meeting of every group. Needless to say, member-led Small Groups were not possible in that church.

It is important for you to support a pastor who either opposes or is neutral toward the idea of a Small Group. If

your pastor says no, then do not start a group in that
church. Offer him or her loving support until the door
opens. If the pastor says, "Okay, but I can't come," or,
"Okay, but I have doubts," proceed cautiously, with con-
sideration for his or her feelings. Ideally, the pastor will be
a part of a Small Group, both to experience it and to model
commitment to the concept of Small Group fellowship.
The pastor will find joy in this because not only will the
group relate to him or her as a leader to be followed but
also as a friend to be supported. If your pastor is not a part
of a Small Group, occasionally invite him to visit your
group; affirm him and pray for him and tell him you are
praying.

When you have gained the necessary approval you will
choose one of two approaches: public or private. Each
approach is effective in beginning a Small Group (and later,
many small groups) in a fellowship or congregation. The
approach you choose depends upon the nature of your particular church or fellowship.

In the private approach you pray daily that God will lead
you to at least one other person or couple who will join you
in Small Group Bible study. The two or three of you may
then pray for and invite more people. Deciding whom to
ask and inviting them is not an easy task. It may take you
weeks, but the work will be worth it. When you have
enough prospects (seven to eleven is good), ask them to
join you for the first meeting. Share the goals and commitments of the group with the prospective members. (A list
of group commitments is given later in this chapter.) With
adults it is often helpful to offer a contract period: "We will
meet once a week for six weeks from 7:00-9:30 P.M. At the
end of that time, we will evaluate our situation. Some or all
of us may continue. Some may leave." This allows people

who are not satisfied with the group to leave without being made to feel like failures.

In the public approach, you invite your whole fellowship or congregation to join in a Small Group. Anyone who wants to join is welcome. Of course, if everyone came, your group would not be small. If more than 10 or 12 sign up, then form two or more groups. When a Small Group grows larger than 12 to 15 people; it becomes a Discipleship Community within which Small Groups need to be organized. (The dynamics of Discipleship Community building are discussed in chapters 10 and 11.)

The public approach is useful if there is a possibility that people might feel excluded if they are not given a chance to participate. Some small congregations, or fellowship communities within a larger church, have a strong sense of being one big family and may resent the idea of a few becoming a separate group. The open invitation allows everyone to feel welcome, and the idea of a Small Group is not as threatening.

A Small Group can be formed entirely of new church members, perhaps as a continuation of a new-member class. However, you must guard against the possibility that these new members will never become assimilated into the church's existing web of relationships. A good way to mix people is to place new members with existing members into Small Groups.

Both the public and private approaches to beginning a Small Group are good. You need to evaluate which method would be best for your fellowship and church in light of your own goals for the group.

Open group or closed group. After a small group is formed, you must decide whether is will be open to new people to come to any meeting or if it will be closed to walk-in participants. The open group welcomes new people to visit and join the group. The closed group stays only with the original members until the determined term of study is complete, then new people my be included by specific invitation. Each method has some advantages.

The open group encourages its members to minister to others by using the With-Me principle to bring outsiders "with" them to the group. It allows others in the church fellowship to feel welcome even if they do not join the group. People in the open group, however, have a more difficult time getting to know each other intimately enough to feel safe about sharing their deep-seated needs. Each time a new person visits, not only does the group have to back up and recap, sharing the situations behind prayer requests and praises, but the trust and confidentiality of the group must be reestablished.

A group that stays closed is able to share much more freely as they become enmeshed in one another's lives. The closed group allows people to develop a high level of trust, confidentiality, and mutual accountability. At the end of a semester of study or any time by consent of the whole group, the closed group may take in new members and let people leave who want to. Then the group closes again for the next term of study. The closed group will not become a clique unless it ministers only to itself. Jesus did not allow the Twelve to become a clique. From the very beginning, He let them know they were to be apostles, which literally means "sent ones." He made it clear that they would serve people outside their own little group. We focus on each other when our Small Group meets and on other people when our group is with other people, such as at the Sunday morning worship service.

The public invitation is always to an open group at

first—any and all are welcome. After the group has formed, it may choose to be a closed group. In a private invitation a person may be invited to join either an open group or a closed group. Private invitation to a person to join an existing closed group should be made only with the consent of every member already in the group.

Designing a Program to Fit the Group

The program of a Small Group meeting may be patterned along with ideas of the Discipleship Triangle (see fig. 1) described in chapter 5. My friend, Jim Walker, introduced this triangle as a pattern for small group life in 1971. Each topic of conversation helps the group members grow in the Three Life-Style Relationships (the Triune God, with the Body of Christ, and with People in the World.)

The Discipleship Triangle is a means of helping the group live the group life-style of Worship (Prayer), Instruction (Word), Fellowship (Share), and Expression (Ministry)—WIFE.

Word. The Small Group spends time sharing insights from Scripture. Even if the group is studying a contemporary Christian book or cassette tapes, Scripture remains the central authority. This is a time when everyone shares insights. It is not a time of formal teaching with a leader doing all the talking. It is a time of sharing so that the network of relationships can grow as everyone enters in on the discussion of Scripture based on what each has learned in personal Bible study during the past week. In this way, each person is encouraged to develop good Bible study habits.

Even if your group chooses to meet for the expressed goal of studying with a teacher, it is important that the teacher teach only one third of the Discipleship Triangle time, leaving plenty of time for discussion and sharing so that relationships will mature and develop. Too often people leave a study group full of information but empty of supportive friendships in the group.

The leaders should study the passage in advance. Since your goal is to get people to share, use your knowledge of the passage to ask questions that will lead them to discover the meaning of the passage and be able to apply it to their real lives. The leader of an effective Bible study focuses on ideas: What does the text mean? and experiences: How does that apply to me or how could it apply to me? Work to keep the balance. Groups that dwell only on ideas, lose the force of how the Scripture applies to their personal lives and group life.

Consider the needs of the individuals in the group when you select a passage of Scripture. If they are new to the Christian faith, talking about how to pray may be more beneficial than a discussion of predestination. If you study a different topic each week, choose a variety of topics that will challenge them to grow in the image of Christ through the New Life, the New MInd, and the New Life-Style (see chap. 3). When a group studies through a book or a portion of the Bible, one passage or paragraph per week, the leader will need to help group members apply the section to their own lives.

As the members sit around a table during study time you may occasionally ask about their Christian life-style with questions like: "How is your personal prayer and Bible study time progressing?" or "Who are you praying for?" or "What is your service to the church?" Such questions are not meant to be a weekly checklist to measure "success"; rather, they are gentle, effective ways to help people think about how they can stretch in their life-style and come closer to conforming to Christ's life-style.

Agree on what time the group will shift from Bible study into sharing and praying, and stick to the schedule. Exciting group Bible discussions that must be stopped to allow time for sharing and prayer actually heighten the anticipation of the next meeting.

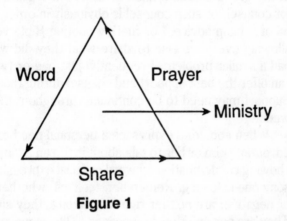

Discipleship Triangle

Word / Prayer

→ Ministry

Share

Figure 1

Share. During sharing time people have a chance to see how God is working in one another's lives each week. They should share their blessings as well as their needs. *Blessings* are what they have seen God do since their last meeting. *Needs* are situations where they want to see God at work. This includes areas where they need encouragement—problems at home, work or health concerns. Often the leader will have to get things going by sharing his or her personal need.

Work to keep this sharing from becoming mechanical or superficial, which can happen if you simply go around the circle mechanically ticking off "a blessing" or "a need." Free sharing is a wonderful experience as people share blessings from God and their own needs in areas where they are experiencing stress, weakness or concern. As a group grows toward maturity, it grows in the mutual trust which each member places in the others and in the depth of their sharing.

Discourage the giving of advice every time a member of the group shares a need or problem. If someone asks for counsel, or such counsel is obviously in order, be careful of "cheap advice," or merely quoting Bible verses, or allowing everyone else to share what they did when they had a similar problem. Frequently, just one or two people can offer the best support and counsel during the meeting. Support may need to be continued throughout the coming week.

When someone expresses a personal need to anxiety, encourage him or her to talk about it. Be an example in not showing condemnation by word or facial expression at how someone is feeling. Remember, feelings, whether positive or negative, are neither right nor wrong, they simply *are*. They are our emotional responses to life as we see it. The group can help a person express anxiety and concern and gently seek the cause of his or her feelings. The feelings may change as they are expressed and as the group helps the person find concrete ways to deal with the reasons behind the feelings.

The Small Group is the place where every person's deepest needs and anxieties can be freely shared. This is especially true for married couples in the group. Often husbands and wives do not share their personal anxieties with each other because they fear criticism. But they can learn to share with each other as they open up to the small, noncritical, supportive group.

Prayer is the third side of the Discipleship Triangle. The group spends time in conversational prayer, an activity that is found in no other support group in society. In prayer the group worships, acknowledging God's presence and honoring Him as God. Teach the group to praise God for His attributes and gifts of love. "Lord, I praise you for your love"; "I praise you for eternal life"; "I praise you for your righteousness." Then the people pray for one another. This is important. Praying for remote concerns such as victims of a famine or earthquake in a distant land certainly are valid, but the Small Group prayer time is more effective if they concentrate on the personal needs of every one in the small group, present or not.

Conversational prayer is where each person converses with God in short prayers, covering no more than one or two requests. Some in the group may pray more than once, some may choose to reinforce the others' prayers silently. Silent periods should be looked upon as worship times, praise times, not concern over who is going to pray next. Someone should be appointed to end the conversational prayer time. He or she should be sensitive to who has prayed and what requests have already been prayed for. That way, every person is given an opportunity to pray and not feel that he or she is *expected* ro pray aloud. The person who closes the prayer time should also mention requests that have not yet been covered.

Evelyn Christenson describes an excellent method of teaching conversational prayer. It consists of six *S*'s, or guides for group prayer.

> Subject by Subject—Pray about one subject or person at a time
> Short Prayers—Not wandering prayers
> Simple Prayers—Not full of high-sounding phrases

Specific Prayer Requests—These are the ones that
have been asked for
Silent Periods—When everyone praises God silently
Small Groups—Best setting for conversational
prayer.[1]

I would add a seventh one: Speak up, since people often
drop their voices when praying aloud and are hard to hear.

Group prayer is a marvelous way that God bonds
together the hearts of people. Fellowship is people with
people with Father and Son (see 1 John 1:3). Prayer time
not only enables worship, but also encourages fellowship.

Ministry, the final portion of our Discipleship Triangle,
occurs first as people in the group minister to one another.
It happens, second, as people in the group minister to people outside the group. As Elton Trueblood stressed in his
book *The Company of the Committed*, the vitality of a
group lies in its ability to gather for strength and disperse
for ministry.

The effective Christian pattern is always a base and a
field. The base—whether it be in a private house or
in a church building—is the center to which the sol-
diers of Christ repair, periodically, for new strength.
The field is the world, and this is where Christians
are supposed to operate . . . . The society of a little
group of fellow believers can be so pleasant that the
poverty and the sorrow of the outside world are forgotten, at least for the time of meeting. But the poverty and the sorrow must never be forgotten, not
even for a little while. A prayer group which does not
make its members more effective apostles in their
jobs and homes, and more sensitive participators in

the fellowship of those who bear the mark of frustration, is essentially a failure. The test of the vitality of a group does not occur primarily while the group is meeting; it occurs after the meeting is over.[2]

Ministry "after the meeting is over," occurs through those who go out from a group meeting to use their gifts in service to those people whom their lives touch. The small group is the most effective place where members can develop the concept that they are commissioned by Christ to serve in "the world" and to build their brothers and sisters in Christ, beginning with the people around them with whom they interact day by day. If, during the Share portion of the meeting, a member shares the name of a person whom God has laid on his heart, and this person is prayed for during Prayer time, often the member who drew attention to the need will feel encouraged by the group to offer personally appropriate ministry to that person.

Ministry beyond the group can also happen as the whole group undertakes a specific mission or ministry project: taking turns seeing that elderly people can get to worship services; helping on clean-up day at the church; hosting an outreach dinner. A group that thinks about the needs in their community will find a task to undertake together.

A small-group evening meeting could follow this suggested format:

7:15 P.M. People gather and chat
7:30 P.M. *Word* (Bible study)
                Sit around a table; read and discuss the passage. Share insights pertaining to the lesson that members have gained from

personal study during the previous week, or what God reveals as the members study the lesson together.

8:15 P.M. *Share*

Members share blessings from God that they have experienced in the past week. Share personal needs in answer to the question, "What one thing do I need prayer for during the coming week?" Share the names of family members, neighbors, or people at work for whom the Holy Spirit has prompted the members to pray.

9:00 P.M. *Prayer*

Pray conversationally. Worship in praise to God and in prayer for people. Everyone in the group is prayed for and has opportunity to pray. Pray for people in one another's lives.

9:30 P.M. Informal chatting in twos and threes. Refreshments. Encourage people members to stay for another half-hour.

10:00 P.M. *Ministry*

People disperse to ministry, to build the people in their families, neighborhoods, and at work in the coming week.

Light refreshments following the Small Group meeting encourages members to stay and chat, enabling the web of relationships to grow. The group should discuss the kinds of refreshments to be served so that everyone knows what is expected of them. Preparation of refreshments should not take the host/hostess out of the group during the meeting.

For an early morning format, the following is an idea:

6:30 A.M. Gather to chat over light refreshments or breakfast
6:45 A.M. Study Bible passage individually
6:55 A.M. Discuss insights from the passage
7:15 A.M. Share prayer requests
7:30 A.M. Pray
7:40 A.M. Dismiss for work or school

Choosing Small Group Commitments

Group unity requires that all members submit to agreed upon ground rules or commitments. A group may choose either to determine its own commitments or to adopt commitments of the larger congregation or organization.

The following commitments have proved useful. Use them "as is" or adapt them for your own small group.

1. *Priority*. Every person will be at the meeting unless prevented by illness or other significant reason.
2. *Punctuality*. The group begins and ends on time.
3. *Confidentiality*. This is crucial. What a person says in confidence is shared in trust. Broken confidentiality is the fastest way to destroy unity, relationships, and ministry.
4. *Prayer*. Pray regularly for the group and for each person in the group by name. Sometimes group members choose prayer partners who pray for each other daily and with each other weekly (often over the phone). Such partners may change every week or every month.

5. *Personal Prayer and Bible study.* Every person will engage in regular Bible study and prayer between group meetings.
6. *No giving of advice* unless counsel is requested.
7. *No arguments.*
8. *Confess your own needs* (not those of other members).
9. *Affirmation and vulnerability.* When we are vulnerable and open ourselves to share deep inner thoughts, feelings, and experiences, we must be in an atmosphere of affirmation. A person who opens up and shares something personal and is then laughed at, ridiculed or criticized may never open up again.

The group may choose to add to or alter these basic commitments. For example, each person may be asked to commit to do specific study assignments. Perhaps they will agree only on the commitments of priority, confidentiality, and prayer. Whatever the group commitments are, everyone in the group should have a copy of them and agree to live by them. If a group invites a new person to join with them, the leader must see that the person understands and accepts the group's commitments.

An on-going Small Group should review its commitments every six months, even if it has met for years. The "Small Group Sheet" in Appendix B may be reproduced as a handout. Simply change the meeting times to suit your group's schedule. In Appendix C is a "Checklist for Starting a Small Group."

In the next chapter we talk about the leadership of the Small Group.

CHAPTER 10

Leading the Small Group

Leading a small group is very rewarding as the leader sees members growing in well-being and discipleship. Personal growth comes about as the Small Group practices the master principles together. It is good to have one or two persons "lead" in the organization and implementation of details of the Small Group. This person, or couple, should be responsible for the overall life and direction of the group, even though week-to-week discussion leadership may be passed around.

If the congregation or fellowship has a Small Group coordinator, which is desirable (we talk about this in the next chapter), the Small Group leader would keep the coordinator informed about his or her group's progress.

The Role of a Leader

Leadership, like any skill, requires some know-how and experience. Following are some guidelines that will help sharpen leadership skills.

Trust God. Understand that this small group belongs to God. It is His work in His people. Expect group members to grow as God uses them individually and as a unit. The leader should trust God to work in his or her life. Pay attention first to God, second to the group. It is easy for a leader to pay so much attention to details of the program that he or she loses sight of God and the people. The leader's goal is to build relationships between God and the members of the group.

Remember the double focus of ministry. The leader should not become so concerned with the group's program and dynamics that he or she loses focus on the individual. The leader should follow up on the members between meetings with phone calls, lunches, recreation. Involve them in ministry.

Assess needs and be flexible. Pray about each person's need and the needs of the group as a whole. Change plans for the program immediately if necessary to meet new needs. Become at ease with the Word/Share/Prayer format, but remember that this formula is a servant to the group, not vice versa. If one person has a special need and the whole program has to be changed to meet that special need, that's OK. Bible study will take place next week. In the ins and outs of regular meetings, the group will spend plenty of time in Bible study, sharing and prayer.

Encourage bonding. The Small Group promotes the Bonding Factors of Unity, Relationships, and Ministry. There are many ways to enhance these factors. I list just a few. These should stimulate your own creative ideas depending on your own church or fellowship.

Unity—Encourage the Bonding Factor of unity:

1. Pray and worship as a group.
2. Sing together.
3. Hold hands during conversational prayer.
4. Eat meals together.
5. Study and share the Word together.
6. Participate in a group task as a ministry.
7. Seek group support in personal hurts and difficulties.
8. Share fun times such as movies, picnics, fairs, with members' families.

Relationships—Build a web of relationships:

1. Share in group discussion.
2. Share in pairs.
3. Invite each other over for meals.
4. Pray together with prayer partners (for each other daily, with each other weekly, in person or by phone).
5. Enjoy refreshments after the meeting.

Ministry—Help people minister to each other:

1. Spend time with one another between meetings.
2. Share responsibilities in the group meetings:
   a. Take turns at leading a meeting.
   b. Help other group members.

    c. Lead singing.
    d. Bring refreshments.
    e. Open your homes for a meeting place.

Continue to ask the two ministry assessment questions: "How can I build each person (person-centered)?" and "How can we build our fellowship as a whole (group centered)?"

Practice the principles personally. PRAY daily for each group member by name; offer appropriate CARE. Make time to encourage the WITH-ME principle in both ministry and leisure. Share the WORD, and SEND-THEM out by encouraging them to minister to each other and with each other.

Have genuine love and concern for each person in the group.

A Guide for the Meetings

Meet weekly; never less than bi-weekly. Less frequently will not allow members to develop in-depth relationships.

Enjoy yourself. In the first meeting, allow people to focus more on getting acquainted than on following the program. Share a meal together at least every two months. God does wonderful things to promote unity and the network of relationships during a meal.

Moderate and guide discussion. A Small Group succeeds when everyone has a chance to share. That means the discussion leader cannot dominate the Bible study time (speak no more than 20 percent of the time), nor can the group leader let any one person dominate the meeting. The following guidelines will help the study leader keep the meeting on course.

1. Keep conversation from wandering too far off the subject. I call this the "rabbit trail." Say to the group, "We're having a great time discussing this, but let's return to our subject; our time is limited."

2. Be vulnerable. Be willing to share your own life so that others may be motivated to respond with their experiences.

3. Allow points of view not in line with your own. Let them be expressed and commented on by others in the group before you respond.

4. Be affirmative, "That's interesting. Have you considered . . . "; do not be negative, "That's wrong."

5. Discourage people interrupting one another. Encourage listening.

6. Control the long-winded speaker. If the discussion leader tends to take too much time teaching, the group leader should insert himself or herself into the speaker's speech: "You've raised a number of good points, John. I'd like to hear some comments from the group on what you've said." Or, between group meetings you could take John aside and say, "John, I've noticed that you have a lot to share with the group when we meet. I appreciate your enthusiasm. I need your help. One of my goals is to get as many people as possible to talk so we can get to know each other. That means that you and I will have to force ourselves to speak less."

7. Encourage the quiet, shy person. "Joyce, what are your thoughts (or feelings) on this?" Or, "Joyce, have you ever experienced something like this?"

8. Be careful how you handle the "stupid" or "heretical" or "unorthodox" comments. Rather than pouncing on the person who made the comment, let the group respond, gently offering a different view. The leader does not have to act as authority on all issues. To avoid argument, some issues are better left unresolved until after the group meeting. The leader can often affirm the speaker: "Bill, you are really thinking through some tough issues. What do the rest of you think about this?"

9. Be sensitive to the emotionally hurt. Sometimes it is appropriate to say, "Jan, what are you feeling now?" Sometimes a group member may simply lay a hand on Jan's shoulder. Obviously, Jan will find more support and healing if the pain or problem is shared. This sharing should be invited, never demanded!

Ask general questions of the group during discussion. If the group is able to discuss a passage without prompting from the leader, good. If there is no response after a reasonable length of time, the leader should not expound it, he or she should ask someone else for an opinion.

Watch the emotional temper of the group. See that no one is being personally attacked. Hurt, anger, and pain need to be acknowledged and validated, not discouraged. Do not be afraid of tears. Encourage people to share their feelings in an atmosphere of support. Help the group to respond with sympathy, not cheap advice.

Involve everyone in group prayer time. Ask different members to open the meetings with prayer; have them take turns beginning and ending conversational prayer.

Help new members learn to pray aloud. Do not make him or her feel pressured. When the person does venture a prayer, affirm him or her by saying, "Thank you for praying for . . . . "

Follow up between meetings. This is a crucial ministry step. Call absent members or see that they are called. Encourage members to call one another and share meals together. Model This. See that the group meets the needs of its members and offers encouragement and comfort. This Person-to-Person ministry is crucial to the maturing of the group. If possible, encourage follow-up "with" someone else, thus building two people at once.

Small Group Commitment: What Are the Ground Rules?

Establish and maintain group commitments. Unity requires that all members submit to the agreed-upon ground rules or commitments. Review the suggested ground rules in chapter 9. Go over these with your group every few months. The group may agree to alter or add to these commitments.

Be sure every member has a copy of the group commitments. They should agree to live by them when they become members of the group.

Encourage accountability. The small group is the ideal

place to maintain group commitments and to grow in any of
the Christian life-style marks. "Joe, your schedule is really
busy. Are you getting enough time with Ann? You're not?
How can we encourage you to spend more time with her
(accountability)?"

The group can hold Joe accountable in several ways.
They may ask, "How was dinner with Ann last week,
Joe?" If Joe did not follow through, he will now! He knows
the group loves him enough to sensitively follow up. If Joe
knows the people in his group will really support him if he
needs and asks for it, he will be much more inclined to follow through with his own growth goals.

Sharing the joys and problems of following various
aspect of the Christian life-style helps to motivate and
train people in their Christian walk.

Never force accountability. You may offer it, or the person may ask for it. "I'm having a rough time setting aside
time for Bible study. Will you hold me accountable to 10
minutes a day?"

More Help for the Leader

Develop new leadership. People learn to lead Small
Groups by leading them. The leader should encourage
members to take turns leading the group. Each meeting
could be led by a different group member. Familiarize him
or her with the Word/Share/Prayer Triangle and the time
schedule. In this way you can develop potential leaders for
future small groups. Even though different people lead
each week, the overall group leader remains responsible
for planning and helping group members to learn to minister to one another.

Be sensitive to a small group's life span. Some Small Groups may last for a comparatively short time. Sometimes people lose their commitment to a group because of a busy personal schedule, because they decided to lead their own Small Groups, or because they feel they would be more comfortable in another group. Sometimes group leaders fear the death of a Small Group as though they had somehow failed. As a result, they will often hang on long after the group has ceased to function in the way it is supposed to.

A leader must help a dissatisfied or underchallenged group member to know that he will be loved, whether or not he remains in the group. If some of the members feel they want to lead their own group, the original Small Group could Send-Them out by laying on hands and pray for them.

If the commitment level of a Small Group falters, or when the contracted weeks of study ends, the leader should encourage a time of open, honest evaluation of the group life. This could be accomplished by having the group share all the ways they have been blessed by God both personally and in the group over the lifetime of the Small Group. These outgoing members should then be encouraged to join other group or form new ones.

Some groups last for years. The members become a lasting support group. We can identify five stages of development for a small group:[1]

1. Getting acquainted
2. Developing trust, unity, a network of relationships
3. Maturing in group life; high commitment
4. Losing of commitment on the part of one or more group members

5. Recommitting and continuing group life or else agreeing to end as a group.

If a group chooses to recommit to another period of time together, some group members may want to leave. They should be allowed to go in total love and support. They should not feel that they are deserting the group or that they have in some way failed in their personal growth. The web of relationships, if it was woven in love and concern, will continue even if some of the people in the web no longer meet together weekly.

A group that ends may decide to meet once or twice a year for a meal. This way, old friendships will continue and the group can grow even closer as they share what has been happening in their lives and pray for one another's future.

Finally, *expect God to build these people and this group*. They are His people, striving to follow His command to "grow in the image of Christ." You partner with God when you continue to ask the two ministry assessment questions: "How can I build each person (person-centered focus)?" and "How can we build our fellowship as a whole (group-centered focus)?" The Holy Spirit will guide you and your people into growth; the Small Group provides a nurturing, encouraging environment for growth to take place. Give yourself in ministry to the group. Trust God for the results.

In the next chapter we will discuss how the Small Group idea can be multiplied in your church or fellowship.

CHAPTER 11

Nurturing a Small Group Movement

One small group can effectively build the active discipleship of its people and provide strong support. However, this effect can be multiplied if more Small Groups are developed. Creating a movement toward establishing and maintaining new small groups must be intentional.

Often a local church looks on Small Groups as a fad or a phase. Several groups will suddenly spring up, almost on their own. People will get excited and lend nominal support; but unless the Body offers ongoing training and encouragement, the Small Group movement will soon fade out of the picture. This is tragic, because the Small Group is where the individual finds significant encouragement to grow toward the image of Christ. It is the place where every person can share his or her deepest needs in confidence, where each one can be encouraged to practice Christian disciplines and find a place to minister.

Your fellowship may have a number of unrelated Small Groups. They may not be part of any Community, but exist independently within your Congregation. Then again, you may have a Community, or several Communities that also have a number of Small Groups such as we will talk about in the next chapter. In this chapter we want to tell how we can nurture a movement toward establishing and strengthening independent Small Groups within your Congregation.

The Control "Center"

Small Group fellowship is essential to ongoing Christian growth; it is not just another church program. Rather, the Small Group fellowship is the place where the personal life-style of the Christian and the life-style of the group is established and sustained. Small Groups must be continually encouraged. Small Groups, however, will not succeed without proper encouragement from leadership.

The first leader who must be behind the Small Group Movement is the *pastor*. The support of the pastor, his or her participation in a Small Group, encouragement from the pulpit, and constant reinforcement of the Small Group as an essential growth opportunity are necessary if the movement is to succeed. He or she is the key person in establishing and continuing a movement of Small Groups.

When a church or fellowship launches the Small Group Movement, it is time to choose a *coordinator*. The Small Group coordinator has three key tasks: (1) to stay in regular contact with each Small Group leader; (2) to offer training for new and continuing Small Group leaders; (3) to help interested people find a Small Group and to help groups find more people.

Many of the coordinator's tasks can be accomplished by meeting with all Small Group leaders every three to six months. Such a meeting enables regular contact, gives an opportunity for more training, and imparts information about which groups need more people or which need to be divided into two groups.

The coordinator should be part of one of the church's ongoing committees or the board, such as the Christian education or adult education committee or the board of elders. Whether the coordinator is appointed to a committee or an existing committee member takes on the job as an additional assignment, *the structure of the church is now responsible for the Small Group movement.* Too often, Small Groups develop as the result of a few who feel the need or because one person generates interest in a few joining him or her in regular meetings. But if the person initially responsible leaves the area or gives up the role for other reasons, and no one else volunteers to replace him or her, the Small Group movement dies. If the responsibility for small groups is assigned to a committee, the coordinator—like the Sunday School superintendent or the stewardship chairperson—will be replaced because the position is essential to the health of the Body. The Small Group coordinator for a Discipleship Community would be a part of the ministry team.

The coordinator of the Small Group Movement should be someone who relates well to people and who has organizational ability. Of course, he or she should be a part of a Small Group.

As we have already mentioned, each Small Group needs a *leader* or a couple as leaders. Leaders of new

Small Groups generally come out of an existing Small
Group. Occasionally, the person who is qualified to lead is
reluctant to leave his or her Small Group because they are
"knit together in love." One way to solve this is to ask the
person or couple to form a new "contract" group. He or
she contracts to lead a new group for six weeks, then
returns to the old group at the end of that time. By six
weeks the new group is well established and can continue
with a leader who has emerged from the new group.

Another way to recruit leaders is to begin a Small
Group with the understanding that after a period of time—
say four months—the group will end and individuals or
couples will lead new groups. People who do not feel
ready to lead a Small Group can team with a leader or
leader couple in starting a new group. The original group
could continue to meet, perhaps quarterly for a meal
together, to sustain relationships.

A third solution is for an existing Small Group to decide
to end so that its members may lead new groups. All of the
new groups commit to meet together in one large group on
a regular basis—twice monthly or quarterly. This time
together insures that people who were knit in friendship in
that first Small Group will continue to see each other often
enough to keep in touch. This approach leads to the Community, which we discuss in the next chapter.

Making More Small Groups

Once you have discovered the value of the Small Group,
you need to create more Small Groups so that more of
your people can grow together in the image of Christ.
There are several ways to start Small Groups. This chapter will suggest five ways: recruit people for them; contract for a limited time; have a retreat or renewal week-

end; divide to multiply; extend the evening service to include Small Group meetings.

Starting new small groups by recruiting members. Actively recruiting members to Small Groups is the basic method of starting new groups. The coordinator could lead a Small Group call-out program, enlisting present members and leaders of existing Small Groups to tell about the blessings they have received since becoming a member of a Small Group. After the call-out, trained leaders should be ready to take names of those who are interested in becoming members of a Small Group. (See Appendix D for a Checklist for starting Small Groups by recruitment.)

The coordinator should develop and maintain a list of people who are interested in becoming part of a Small Group. These names may come from the people themselves, from the coordinator or the pastor, from response to a congregational Small Group call-out announcement, or from Small Group leaders. The list should never get very long because the coordinator will continue to get people together, arrange for leadership, and form new groups.

Get people to contract to meet for a specific number of weeks. People who have never experienced a Small Group can often be persuaded to try out one if it meets for a short time around a specific theme or subject. The coordinator, in cooperation with a Small Group leader, could select a short Bible study on a specific topic, some published study material, or a church-wide six-week Fall or lenten series. People would be encouraged to sign up—contract—for a six-week study. The leaders may be someone on temporary leave from his or her own Small Group. Some people will respond better if they know they only have to be committed for a limited number of weeks.

Hopefully, by the end of six, eight, or ten weeks, most of the people will recognize how their lives are growing in the Small Group and will continue.

At the end of the six—week period, the coordinator seeks those who would be interested in continuing in a small group. The contracted group leader is then free to return to his or her own group, or remain with the new group. Perhaps someone in the new group is gifted in leadership and would take training to become a leader.

Have a retreat or renewal weekend for the purpose of introducing Small Groups. A particularly effective way to introduce the Small Group Movement to your church or fellowship for the first time is to have a renewal weekend at the church or at a conference center. Begin on Friday evening with a speaker, a lay renewal team or a seminar leader. People are then asked to form Small Groups and continue discussion. This could be repeated on Saturday morning. The groups should use the Word/Share/Prayer format in their Small Groups. A core of leaders could already be trained to lead these impromptu groups, or, as often is the case, out of each group someone will volunteer or be appointed by the group to "take charge" of the Word/Share/Prayer time. During this renewal weekend the participants are invited to sign up for a Small Group that will continue to meet for a six-week trial period. After the initial six weeks, the people may be given the opportunity to continue meeting. These groups would be led by trained leaders. (See Appendix E.)

Multiplying the number of Small Groups by dividing. It is also possible to get a Small Group of potential leaders to meet together for six months, then divide and form two, three or more groups and lead them. When they first divide they would seek out new members to join each group who will commit to the Small Group ground rules. Of course, such a plan would have to be clear from the beginning. Those who originally join such a group would understand that the purpose is to form more Small Groups with them as leaders at the end of a specified period of time. Even though everyone understands this, sometimes it is difficult to break up at the end of the six-month period because they have become knit together. The original group could continue to meet together every three months in order to renew their friendships and discuss the joys and problems they are having with their own new groups (always keeping the confidence of the new group.)

Eventually, the process of multiplying Small Groups by dividing will slow down because people in second and third generation groups will be less committed to dividing and will want to stay together. However, even if only two or three generations develop, there are that many more people now growing in Small Groups. (See Appendix F.)

Extend the evening service to include Small Group meetings. Another way to build a Small Group Movement is to add groups to an existing church program during the week or to the Sunday evening worship hour. Right after the service, people could disperse to homes for Small Group meetings. The format would be the same: Discuss the Word (the text which was preached at the service that just ended), share needs and blessings, and pray. Sunday School classes are sometimes ideal for forming Small Groups. The people in the classes could meet together during the week for the Word/Share/Prayer small group.

The Small Group movement can work in nearly any church or ministry setting. It is a highly effective means of building people since it places them in a caring and disciple building environment. For a successful movement of Small Groups the ministry will need (1) the support and participation of the pastor, (2) a coordinator, (3) trained or experienced group leaders, and (4) a plan for forming new groups.

In the Appendix section of this book are checklists for forming Small Groups which you may use as they appear or change to fit your particular church or ministry.

CHAPTER 12

Forming the Discipleship Community

In chapter 6 I described the nesting structure of a ministry (see fig. 1). I then identified a Small Group as consisting of up to 12 people and a Discipleship Community numbering between 12 and 250, with the larger "nest" being the Congregation. This chapter describes the forming and activities of the Discipleship Community. Both large and small congregations may have such communities within them.

A Discipleship Community is open to anyone who is concerned with personal growth. Of course, every church is a discipleship Community in the broadest sense; here, however, the community refers to the size of a group. The goal of the Discipleship Community is to build the individuals and the Small Groups as a whole in the image of Christ.

The Discipleship Community differs from the Small Group in many ways. They are similar in that they both offer the Body of Christ significant opportunities for growth. But the Community can add a vital component to the life of a growing Christian.

A Discipleship Community excels in:	A Small Group excels in:
Many relationships	Intimacy
Welcoming new people	Deepening relationships with a few
High Inspiration	High Support
Sense of togetherness	Accountability
Formal teaching	Discussion
	Sharing of personal lives

The Discipleship Community acts as a "generating center" for starting new Small Groups. It is a place where new people can participate comfortably in a non-threatening environment until they enter Small Groups. It is a place where fear and apprehension of a Small Group can be overcome. It offers a place for people to belong, whether or not they ever become a part of a Small Group.

Nested within the Congregation, the Discipleship Community and its Small Groups offer people the strongest expression of the bonding factors of unity, relationships, and shared ministry. The community is always "open" and provides a gathering to which members may bring friends, using the With-Me principle. (A community that is not open to new people, either deliberately or inadvertently, develops a closed network of relationships, becoming a single cell which will ultimately stifle growth of

Components of the Spectrum of Ministry

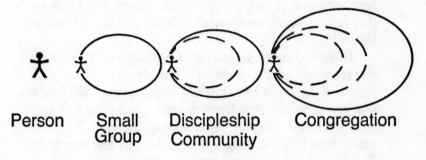

| Person | Small Group | Discipleship Community | Congregation |

Figure 1

the individual and the group.) The Discipleship Community
enables personal growth because it offers an arena for formal teaching.

Jesus' Discipleship Community were those large
groups of people who followed Him because they were
hungry for the Word (His Small Group being the Twelve,
and His "few" being the three, Peter, James and John).
People become part of a community for various reasons:
some join because they respect the leader; some join to be
near someone already in the group; others join because
they have a basic commitment to being part of a Christian
fellowship.

There are many variations of a Discipleship Community meeting. Imagine walking into a room filled with people, some sitting, a few standing, most talking. You find a
seat and soon someone leads the group in a song that lifts
your spirit and builds a sense of expectation. Then the
leader launches into a vigorous, well-paced teaching from
Scripture. After teaching, singing, and prayer, the people
disperse to homes to continue in Small Groups to study
the Bible, share needs and blessings, and to pray for one
another (Word/Share/Prayer). This Community offers
inspiration, solid teaching, Small Group fellowship and is
open to all comers.

In another variation the community might divide into
Small Groups and stay at the church. After a time of study,
sharing, and prayer, the whole group gathers again for a
time of worship. A third variation would have the community meet in Small Groups at one time, and for service to
the community or the Body at another—such as choir
rehearsal, visitation evangelism, or a neighborhood ministry project. There are infinite numbers of variations, but
Discipleship Communities need to follow a certain pattern
and use biblical principles of ministry if they are to build

people in Christ successfully. Basic to the building process is the nesting of the Small Groups within the large one. (See fig. 1.)

In this chapter we will discuss two ways to start a Discipleship Community: (1) Organizing from Scratch; (2) Reorganize an Existing Community, and How to Plan the Program. In the next chapter we will talk about the Leadership of the Discipleship Community.

Organizing from Scratch

A Discipleship Community may either start from scratch or be reorganized from an existing meeting. We will describe the three stages of a "start from scratch" Discipleship Community first. The advantage of being able to start a brand new community from scratch is that you can make it a weekly happening right from the start. A community that is already established may be a monthly meeting whose people are not ready to change. How do you start a Discipleship Community in a fellowship that has never had one?

Stage One: By Public Invitation. Jesus used public invitations to build His Discipleship Community. He began by inviting all who wished to join HIm as He led in teaching large crowds that gathered at His invitation.

Publicly invite anyone and everyone to join you in a group that will meet each week to study the Bible and for fellowship. In a church, such an invitation would be made publicly to all members and privately to individuals (come with me). This idea also would work if you wanted to start a Discipleship Community in your neighborhood, apartment complex, or college campus by making your invitation known there.

If at first, 12 or fewer people respond to your invitation, then you may choose to develop a Small Group or a Small Group Movement. If enough people respond to create a Discipleship Community, ask two or three people to join you in a preliminary ministry team (see chap. 13). You and the ministry team will begin the process of WIFE—Worship, Instruction, Fellowship, and Expression.

Stage 2: Ministry team invitations. During the entire life of the Community, you, as the leader, continue to pray the people-building prayers: "Lord, who do you want with me?" and "Who do you want me to focus on?" Who are the people God wants to join with you in community? Jesus, after He had begun an open Community, prayed all night before He selected the Twelve from the community (Luke 6:12). You too need to pray about the few from the community who will be your ministry team. They will grow with you in discipleship and seek to build the wider Discipleship Community. Some churches require that leadership teams be elected rather than invited. Either way, the goals of the team are the same.

An important step in this stage is when you are able to appoint someone on your ministry team as a Small Group coordinator. The coordinator in turn seeks out people who will train to become Small Group leaders.

Stage 3: Small Groups. As God leads people to join the community in response to your open invitation, there will be some who already have the experience necessary to lead Small Groups; others will need to be trained to lead a Small Group. Members of the ministry team may start out being Small Group leaders; however, as the movement grows, other people will have to be enlisted to lead other groups. These Small Groups may choose to meet right after the Discipleship Community meets, or they may choose another time.

Not everyone who joins the community will want to be in a Small Group. Some will be uneasy about the idea and others will have schedule problems; however, the people are still members of the Discipleship Community. Eventually, they may feel comfortable about becoming a part of a Small Group.

The Small Group leaders are accountable to the leader of the Discipleship Community. They should meet regularly—at least every six months, if not more frequently—with this leader or a Small Group coordinator for training (see chap. 10), mutual support, and direction as they share the needs and joys of the group as a whole (not the confidences of the individuals). If the community has many Small Groups, there may be too many for a group meeting to be effective; the coordinator may have to ask other ministry team members to focus on just a few Small Group leaders.

Generally, these three stages of starting a Discipleship Community may take only a few weeks or it may take a year or more. A typical new community might meet weekly for three or four months before the leader begins to know which people should be challenged to join a ministry team. If possible, start a community with two or three people who will serve with you on a preliminary ministry team. Soon you will agree on who else to invite onto the team. The community may have only one or two Small Groups in the early stages. The number will grow as the Small Group concept is understood and accepted.

These three stages (fig. 2) are not expected to be slavishly followed; they are an illustration of the development process. Every developing Discipleship Community will experience these stages at some point; however, change and order and overlapping are not unusual. For example, it would be to the community leader's advantage to have someone else on the leadership team from the beginning; or the community may have Small Groups before the ministry team is formed.

Reorganizing an Existing Community. Starting new Discipleship Communities is not always an option in a church or Christian organization if there are already several existing communities—such as men's fellowship, women's fellowship, youth groups, singles groups, and so forth. Rather than suddenly changing an organizational structure that already provides some support for the members, which could threaten group members, begin by adding Person-to-Person ministries and Small Group meetings to these existing communities, then encourage the Small Groups to meet together weekly.

Deciding how often the community and Small Groups meet requires taking into account many factors. A group must meet regularly, with not too many days between, if the web of relationships is going to grow. All the Bonding Factors of Unity, Friendship, and Shared Ministry are stronger when the group meets weekly. Twice a month will work, but monthly is really not enough. Monthly meetings are fine for instruction and worship but are inadequate in helping real friendships to form.

A group of busy adults will probably not be able to meet more than one night a week for teaching and fellowship; therefore, you must offer both large and Small Group experiences on the same night. High school or college/career young people can often meet once a week in a large group and on a different night in Small Groups. The more often Small Groups meet, the stronger will be the Bonding Factors.

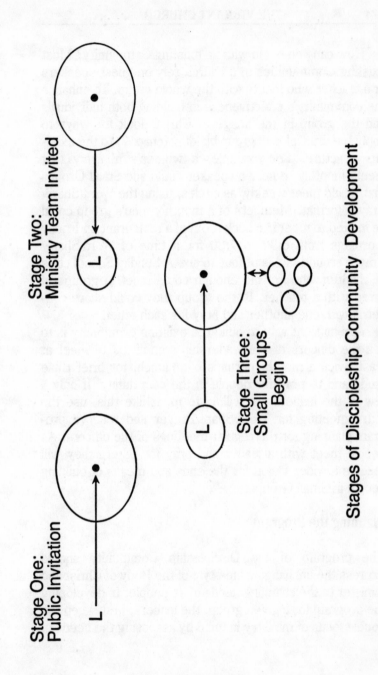

Stage One:
Public Invitation

Stage Two:
Ministry Team Invited

Stage Three:
Small Groups
Begin

Stages of Discipleship Community Development

Figure 2

How can you begin with an existing Community? Most existing Communities in a church rely on guest speakers or a teacher who meets with the whole group. To enhance the community's effectiveness in building both individuals and the group in the image of Christ, look for ways to apply the principles of group building (chap. 7) to the existing structure. For example, a women's ministry that meets monthly to hear a speaker could add Small Groups that would meet weekly, as circles, using the Word/Share/Prayer format. Members of a monthly men's group could be invited to meet in a back room of a restaurant on Friday mornings from 6:30 to 7:30 for a time of Word/Share/Prayer around tables of four to six. A Sunday School class of children who are old enough could meet in groups of three with a teacher. In the group they could share concerns with one another and pray for each other.

A significant way to build the existing community is to ask the officers of the leadership committee to meet at least twice a month, perhaps over lunch, for brief Bible study and to pray for people in the community. If only a few of the leaders are willing to meet like this, use the extra meeting for Word/Share/Prayer and reserve program planning for the regular meetings of the officers. As people meet with a leader and pray for others they will receive a wider vision for the ends and means of building people in Small Groups.

Planning the Program

The program of the Discipleship Community should express the unchanging life-style of the Body of Christ and minister to the changing needs of its people. In developing the program for a given group, the leaders, first, keep the double focus of ministry in mind by assessing the needs of the individuals in the group and the needs of the group as a whole (such as the status of the Bonding Factors). Second they review the principles of ministry: Prayer, Care, With-Me, Word, Send-Them. Then they develop a program that addresses both the individual and the corporate needs of the people and also uses the principles of ministry.

The program ideas we have included are only a sampling of ways to conduct a program for your community. You should select one that will enable you to express corporate life-style and also build the members. Even though the life-style (WIFE) is universal to Christian groups, the different methods and ways of expressing that life-style will vary from group to group. The more elements of life-style we build into a group the more vibrant its life will be.

A successful Discipleship Community meeting regularly *gathers* the community together and *disperses* the community into Small Groups. The Discipleship Community/Small-Group activities may take place in a single meeting or the Small Groups could meet at different times and locations. The following are some community schedule variations.

The basic community meeting (see fig. 3). In this schedule the entire Discipleship Community gathers at church or in a home or other meeting place each week.

First, begin the WIFE structured meeting with *Instruction* from the Word. This should be a time of challenging, fast-paced, uplifting Bible study that grips the mind and heart. You could use lecture, discussion, or any method the leader—teacher feels will generate enthusiasm and love for Scripture so that the people will be motivated to make the study of Scripture part of their personal lives between community meetings. Set a time limit for Instruction—30 to 45 minutes. Be sure to leave at least

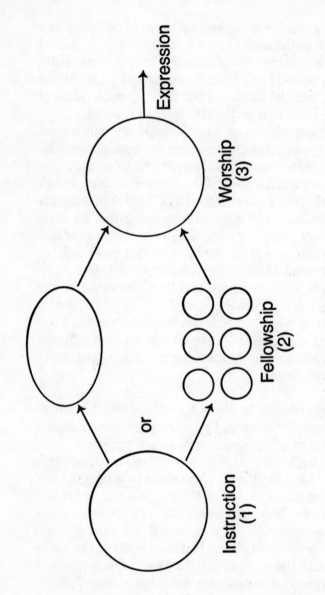

Instruction
(1)

or

Fellowship
(2)

Worship
(3)

Expression

Basic Community Meeting

Figure 3

half of the meeting time for Fellowship and Worship. Remember, the goal of Discipleship Community is not just to teach content, but to build relationships with the Triune God, with the Body of Christ, and with people outside the group.

Second, at the appropriate time begin *Fellowship*—the sharing of personal blessings and needs. This sharing could take place either with the entire group or when they divide into Small Groups. Fellowship builds as people grow in love for one another personally and for the group as a whole. This happens most effectively during the meeting when people have the opportunity to share their blessings from God and their needs for prayer. In this sharing, the people talk to each other, recognize God's blessings, and experience support from God's people.

The people may share their needs with the entire group or in Small Groups of four to six. If you regularly share in Small Groups, once in a while you could stay together in the large group to share blessings and any needs which members feel like revealing so that everyone can experience God's working and sense the oneness of the community. But breaking into Small Groups is still most effective in forming friendships and providing a place where the quieter people can feel free to share, and where sensitive or confidential needs can be expressed and prayed for. If people share blessings and prayer requests with the whole group, allow 15 minutes or so. If they break into groups of six or more, give them 30 minutes.

Third, the entire community gathers together for a closing time of *Worship*. God's greatest means of building fellowship and unity is worship. Our greatest means of honoring Him is worship. Designing an effective time of worship will take much prayer, planning, and experimenting with your group. The key is to find a blend of music, prayer, Scripture, and silence that really brings the people into an awareness of God's presence and leads them to honor Him. The worship leader (who may be the Discipleship Community leader or another member of the worship team) works to find a worship pattern that will bless the people and bless the Lord.

The final part of our WIFE format, *Expression* (outreach) and fellowship of the Community, may occur in periodic social fellowship events, such as dinners and fun nights. These events offer the opportunity of extending and deepening the group's web of relationships and also provide a place where members can bring uninvolved Christians and non-Christian friends. Also, this is a time when plans can be made for compassion and evangelism projects in the local neighborhood.

How these four Life-Style Marks fit into a Discipleship Community program is illustrated below. This basic four-part schedule can be adapted to a variety of Community variations:

Evening Community	*Women's Community*	*Men's Community*
7:00 P.M.	9:30 A.M.	6:30 A.M.
Instruction	Instruction	Instruction
7:45 P.M.	10:15 A.M.	7:00 A.M.
Fellowship	Fellowship	Fellowship
8:30 P.M.	11:00 A.M.	7:30 A.M.
Worship	Worship	Worship
9:00 P.M.	11:30 A.M.	7:45 A.M.
Dismiss	Dismiss	Dismiss

Figure 4 gives a detailed look at the basic community meeting showing the ministry team's role (1), the ministry function of the informal times before and after the meeting

"THE MEETING"

Ministry Team (1)	Fellowship (2)	Instruction (3)	Fellowship (4)	Worship (5)	Fellowship (6)	Small Group (7)	Ministry (8)
Touch Base: How are we?	People begin to come and mix	Teaching the Word	Share in large group or small groups:	Praise	People Mix	May meet after big group or at other times	Follow Up during week:
Double Focus	Focus on People	by lecture, discussion, etc.	Where do you see God at work?	Music	Focus on People	Word	Appointments
People: Who Is Coming?	Seating		Blessings	Who He Is	Refreshments Occasionally	Share	Phone Calls
Any Special Needs?	Music—upbeat		Needs	What He Has Done and Does		Prayer	Lunches
Who Will Focus on Whom?	Welcome		If in small groups, pray on behalf of one another before joining large group	Prayer			Prayer in 2s
Program: What is to happen?	Prayer			Needs of Saints and of Group Needs of World			
Who will do what?							

Discipleship Community Schedule

Figure 4

(2) and (6), and the ministry that can be going on in each of the sections (4) of the schedule. Notice that the times of fellowship before and after the "meeting" are key parts of the Discipleship Community gathering, not just "filler" time, waiting for the meeting to start or for people to go home. The ministry team actively uses this time for Person-to-Person ministry, welcoming new people, encouraging regular members.

Refreshments may be served during the fellowship time after the Worship (5) segment unless the community disperses immediately to homes for Small Groups. Refreshments encourage people to stand around and talk, enhancing the chances for the web of relationships to grow.

Basic community meeting ending with Small-Group sharing. In this schedule the community gathers each week for teaching and worship, then disperses to Small Groups in homes for the remainder of the evening (or morning or afternoon) for fellowship. The people may also remain in the church, large home, or meeting room, forming Small Groups in other rooms or in corners of the same large room. A suggested schedule for this format would be:

7:00   Community gathers for Instruction and Worship.
8:00   Community disperses to Small Groups.
8:15-9:30 Small Groups in home if possible.

This is a terrific schedule if the community is made up of busy people who may have limited time to give. It offers an open-group opportunity for new people when the community meets at the church, and also offers Small Group intimacy and accountability. People can receive teaching in the large group and share what they are personally learning from Scripture in the Small Group. This schedule allows people to share the warmth of their homes and to practice hospitality.

The advantage to this schedule is that it not only gives weekly exposure to the entire community, but it offers more time for Small Groups to meet. Its disadvantages are the tightness of the schedule and the limited time for fellowship in the large group. One solution is to have the Discipleship Community have a longer meeting every six to ten weeks, perhaps in a home, for a time of refreshment, some mixers, and a brief time of encouragement from the leader. The community meeting could last an hour extra, but Small Groups would not follow it.

This schedule works well for a men's or women's group meeting in a restaurant where people sit in Small Groups of four to six at tables. The whole group sings together and studies the Word. Then the remainder of the meeting is spent in Word/Share/Prayer over a meal at the tables.

In a city where homes are distant or scattered throughout the city, it is easier and takes less travel time if the Small Groups meet at church following a community meeting. Or, people who live in the same geographical area, within 15 minutes of one another, could meet in a home in their area, and so forth around the city.

Evening worship service plus Small Groups. An adaptation of the preceding plan is that the evening worship service could be considered a gathering of the Discipleship Community, followed by Small Group gatherings after the service. This would necessitate an evening worship service of no longer than one hour, from 7:00 to 8:00 P.M. for example. The people receive Worship and Instruction at the evening service, than meet in Small Groups afterwards in homes or at the church for continued study and fellowship.

Sunday morning Bible study classes plus Small Groups. Many churches have Sunday School classes that follow a format similar to the basic community meeting. The impact of this Bible study time can be increased if people in the classes meet during the week in home Bible study and fellowship. The same could apply to a Wednesday night Bible study to which home Small Groups are added.

Community and Small Groups meet at different times. This format gives maximum time to both the large and Small Groups, but it is not as easy to follow if yours is a busy church with many meetings (Sunday morning and evening worship, midweek Bible study, etc.). However, if it is possible to hold a community meeting on Wednesday night, for example, from 7:00 to 8:00 P.M., then Small Groups could meet on any other night (or day) which the members can agree on. This is a useful schedule for youth groups and collegians whose personal schedules may permit more opportunities to meet. Adult choirs are communities that meet once a week for rehearsal, so would need to schedule Small Groups at a different time.

Community every other week, Small Groups on alternate weeks.[1] The community would meet every other week from 7:00 to 9:00 P.M., using the basic community meeting format (fig. 3). On alternate weeks, people from the community would meet in Small Groups in homes, if possible, beginning at 7:00 or 7:30. The advantage of this schedule is that it gives a full evening to both the Discipleship Community and the Small Group experience. The disadvantage is that it takes longer for people to develop deep relationship, meeting in Small Groups only every other week. However, if the same people meet together faithfully throughout the year, they can overcome this disadvantage. In this schedule, people may become more committed to their Small Group than to the community. It is a good schedule for people who live quite a distance from one another.

Visitation evangelism as a community. Many churches have a visitation evangelism ministry. This ministry is actually a Discipleship Community whose mission is evangelism. In the meeting the whole group gathers for a brief time of instruction and prayer. Then teams of two or three (Small Groups) leave to visit in homes. Afterwards all Small Groups return to the community gathering place for a brief time of sharing, debriefing, and prayer. Such a ministry may effectively use all of the principles of building people, thus generating spiritual growth.

Consider the community meeting room. The physical surroundings in which a group meets plays a significant role in the group's experience. For example, 50 people crowded into a small room will have a much greater sense of unity and excitement than the same 50 meeting in a huge sanctuary. Someone nicknamed this the "herd" principle. Of course, you will have to spread out into other rooms or even outside if you break into Small Groups in the same facility. If you meet in a very large room, using various screening devices will create a sense of closeness.

Consider the seating in the room. Seat people as close together as is practical and comfortable. Pay attention to the temperature of the room. When a room is too hot or too cold, people lose interest in the community's activities. Minimize distracting noises from outside the room, such as children playing and people talking. Small Group meetings are often enhanced by gathering in homes. Not only does a home offer warmth, but the host has an opportunity to practice hospitality. Small Groups will find that sitting around a table intensifies their discussion. People are relaxed, and the table helps them feel involved and attentive. Wherever you meet, seek to help people be comfortable.

Notice that all the schedule variations use the principle of nested groups: a large group meeting, the Discipleship Community; Small Group Bible studies; a ministry team; and of course the individual.

Choose a time for community meetings that best fit the existing calendar of your church or fellowship. Choose times that best fit the schedules of the people you want to reach. For example, working men or women's groups would have to meet before 8:00 A.M.; a couple's group at night; a women's group in the morning.

Choose a schedule that will best help your people experience both the large group and Small Group elements of the community. You may have to experiment before you find a schedule that feels right. You may have different schedules for different groups.

The Discipleship Community is an open group, allowing everyone who wants to be involved to do so. Community building is not always easy. Many variables, such as the openness of people to participate, the quality of leadership, and the willingness of people to build their network of relationship—will determine how the community will grow and how successful it becomes at helping to conform people to the image of Christ.

If you seem to be having difficulty in building a community, ask the person-centered and group-centered ministry assessment questions and evaluate other aspects of the program. One community I started grew from 18 people the first year to 16 people the second! However, the lessons we learned from that effort helped us start a new group that grew from 30 to 100 in three years. In Appendix G is a checklist to help you develop a Discipleship Community.

In the next chapter we will talk about the ministry team.

CHAPTER 13

Developing a Ministry Team

The ministry team, the leaders of the Discipleship Community, can be one of the most effective and successful of the Small Groups. Members of the ministry team have potentially the most satisfying opportunities, first, to build each other on the team, and second, to offer leadership to the community in a double focus of ministry (see fig. 1).

Eventually, the community will need (1) a Discipleship Community leader; (2) a Small Group coordinator; (3) Small Group leaders. A Congregation may have several Communities (see chap. 14), each one having its own ministry team. In this chapter we will talk about What Kind of Person Should Be on the Ministry Team? How Is a Ministry Team Developed? and What Makes up a Typical Ministry Team Meeting?

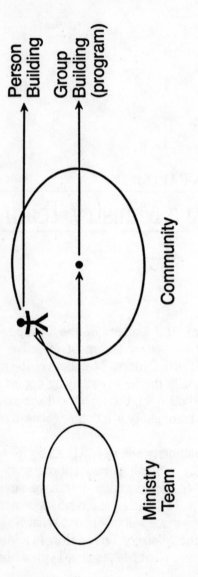

Ministry Team in a Double Focus of Ministry

Figure 1

What Kind of Person Should Be on the Ministry Team?

Whether your church or fellowship is just starting a Discipleship Community or the leadership is going to develop a community from an existing organization, the first order of business is to acquire a Discipleship Community leader. Typically, this person is on the church staff or is a mature loyal member who has the gifts of leading, pastoring, and teaching. A church or fellowship may elect members of the ministry team, or the Discipleship Community leader may select those who will serve with him or her. Whether the ministry team of your church or fellowship is elected or chosen, there are certain basic criteria which those responsible for forming the group should follow.

1. Since the members of the ministry team both model and teach the life-style of the Body of Christ, it is wise to seek people who are already growing in Christ, showing that they have a heart first for God and second a heart for people. Sometimes a person may have a heart for God but has never been exposed to Person-to-Person ministry. However, this is something that can be taught.

2. Since they will be led, and often built, by the team leader, members should be teachable by that leader. Sometimes, Christians have a profound heart for God and for people but simply will not learn from or follow a leader. Such people can cause constant conflict within a team because they do not cooperate with the team.

3. Since they will often be called on to meet with the team, to focus on people, and to encourage community life-style, ministry team members should be available. It is no use having a heart for God and for people, and being teachable, if they are so busy they cannot give themselves wholeheartedly to the team and its work.

Finding such people in the early formation of the Discipleship Community may be difficult, but as those in the community begin to grow in Christ, more and more of them will become qualified to serve on a ministry team.

How can you know if a person meets these qualifications? Often you cannot; only God truly knows the motives of the heart. The best way to find out where people are in their spiritual maturity is to spend time with them. Get to know them personally. Of course, the above checklist is only a guide. There is often a bit of mystery as to why the Holy Spirit leads you or your group to select team members. God is very much a part of the process. The leader must be sensitive to God's leading and choose people who want to serve and with whom he or she can work.

When a person on the ministry team lacks the double focus of ministry, he or she tends to have a purely program focus. "Who will set up the chairs? Get refreshments? Lead singing?" The leader must encourage purely program-minded people to think about people's needs.

Never ask someone to take a leadership role in a group in order to help that person become more involved. Giving Joe a job so that "maybe he'll be more active" can be disastrous. Joe may or may not get more active, and his leadership office could go untended. It is important to choose people to lead who have already proven themselves in a personal ministry.

If you are starting a Discipleship Community from an existing group, you may not have the privilege of selecting a leadership team. In that case, the leader could gather an informal "caring hub" that meets together briefly before and after a community meeting to discuss people's needs and initiate follow-up ministry between meetings. Such a caring hub ideally would include some of the elected officers of the group; if not, then the existing officers need to

understand what this caring hub is all about. Since the officers already carry the program responsibilities for the
community, they should be made to understand that this
Small Group who meets with a leader is a "people-team,"
whose focus is to minister to people in one-on-one and
small-group ministry. If the people team desires to initiate
a Small Group program or a ministry, then they will need
to win the support and the endorsement of the existing
officers. The people team needs to help the officers see
that they are there to support and not compete with the
program.

How Is a Ministry Team Developed?

There are three stages in developing a ministry team, and
a final stage in assuring that the program continues to be
effective.

Stage 1: the ministry team is recruited. If the ministry
team is to be elected, the leader needs to encourage the
nominating committee to seek out people who meet the
qualifications we listed and recommend names of such
people to the nominating committee. Elected leaders usually see themselves as elected to the leadership team but
not necessarily to personal commitment to the leaders and
others on the team. Perhaps it will be necessary for the
leader to meet with each elected member and talk about
his or her commitment to Christ and personal commitment
to one another and ministry to the group. We are modeling
Jesus' principle to invite people to be with Him, personally,
in ministry. Maybe the leader could establish a prayer
partnership between each elected member and himself/
herself.

If the leader of the community has the freedom to

select the team, he or she should regularly pray the prayer of selection: "Lord who do you want on this team? Who do you want me to focus on?" even as Christ prayed all night before appointing the Twelve (Luke 6:12). Then, with the others on the team, the leader prayerfully considers the members of the Discipleship Community and their qualifications for becoming members of the team. These will not be merely leaders on a committee, but will be those who are responsible for building people. This should be emphasized as each person is chosen.

If the leader is starting out with no ministry team, he or she should begin by choosing one person to be "with me as, together, we commit ourselves to Jesus Christ." Then the two will work and pray together about asking more people to join them, thus beginning a ministry team. As the leader invites others to join with the "few," he or she will ask, "Pat, will you pray about committing yourself to me as I will commit myself to you and then together we will commit ourselves to Jesus Christ, to the others on the ministry team, and finally to our ministry to the Discipleship Community?" As the team grows, the responsibility for selecting further team members becomes a matter for the whole team. Yet, it remains the leader's task to actually invite new people onto the team. Jesus Christ asked the Twelve to be with Him, and so we ask people to be "With-Me" in service of Christ and His people.

By using this method of recruitment, ministry team members become bonded by commitment to each other (Relationships) and to the whole team (Unity). Members of the team understand that they will be a Small Group, personally committed to the leader and to each other. At first, they meet primarily for their own support; as they grow together in unity, then they can begin to operate as a ministry team to the whole community.

There is no "right size" for a ministry team, although 10 to 12—the recommended size for a small group—is about as big as a team can be without requiring sub-groups of its own. If you are the leader, do not be pressured to find 12, simply because Jesus had the Twelve. Rather, pray that God will lead you to those who best meet the criteria we described earlier in the chapter. A small ministry team of people who love God and people, are teachable, and are available is far more effective than a team of one dozen whose members are not in tune with the direction or unity of the rest of the team and its leader.

Whenever a ministry team is finally selected by the leader, he or she should be careful about "springing" them on the rest of the community. Since each person on the team was personally invited to join, there was no fanfare to alert the community about the ministry team. The leadership should be sensitive and avoid the possibility of people feeling left out because they were not asked to join the privileged few. Eventually, the community will have to be made aware of this small group of people who have been praying for them and for their corporate and individual ministries. They will begin to understand that the purpose of the ministry team is for continued growth of the community, and that team members will be as available as the leader is to help members of the community who need support.

Stage 2: The ministry team as a Small Group. The ministry team will begin meeting as a support group, using the Small Group meeting format Word/Share/Prayer described in an earlier chapter. The leader will exercise the double focus of ministry on the team, seeking to build individuals and to encourage the Bonding Factors and the corporate life-style (WIFE) of the team itself. The ministry team will continue to be a caring group as the leader moves the team into its next stage of development: ministry in the community along with the leader.

Stage 3: The ministry team begins their double focus. In early ministry stages, the leader, and perhaps a few key ministry team people, will plan the program of the community meetings with Worship, Instruction, Fellowship and Expression (WIFE) and will build the Bonding Factors. He or she will ask the ministry assessment questions (chap. 9) and plan the program according to the resulting answers. The leader can involve the team in some of these program decisions, but at this stage the goal is to get them to *spend time with people* in the community. The ministry team must see themselves primarily as people-focused rather than program-focused. Since the going thing in churches today is to develop and attend programs, people-building must be developed in team members before they are burdened with permanent program responsibilities, such as music leader, Small Group coordinator, and so forth. Each team member must see himself and herself as sent to serve the needs of people in the Discipleship Community and to use their gifts in service to the group.

Of course, the leader will need to ask members of the ministry team for specific help in the administrative aspects of a program: "John, will you set up the chairs? Phyllis, will you get the refreshments? And we'll need your guitar, Bill"; but such program details should not be taken care of during ministry team meetings unless they are things which demand the entire team's input.

As the team develops rapport as a Small Group, the leader will begin to include more time in focusing on people during the team meetings. To do this, the leader may have to train team members in Person-to-Person ministry and Small Group ministry. Figure 2 shows how a leader ministers with another team member to someone in the community, while other team members minister in twos to other people in the community. The practice of sending people to minister in twos is the way Jesus often did it (see Mark 14:13; Luke 10:1; 19:29).

Ministry Team Focusing on People

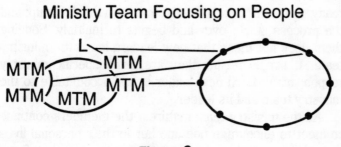

Figure 2

Notice in the figure that one team member (MTM) is not ministering to anyone; another is ministering alone. Encourage ministering in twos; but it does not always happen that way. In this figure the ministry team is now ministering to the community during and between the community meetings in Person-to-Person ministry. Occasionally, team members will attend a meeting of the Discipleship Community and not focus ministry on anyone because they need encouragement and support themselves. This is all right; the fellowship is a place where every person can both give and receive.

The ministry team discusses the results of these efforts. The leader teaches team members to trust God to work in people's lives; the leader's prayer is that the members will develop their own heart for people and initiate their own Person-to-Person ministries (chaps. 4 and 5). The Small Group meetings of the ministry team is the place to discuss how well each person is learning to build people. The team learns to focus on people during and between community gatherings.

As team members begin to lead out in the Small Group meeting, their people-focused ministry starts to expand. When the leader senses that a team member or couple is ready, the team "Sends Them" to start a Small Group; and the process starts over and begins to multiply. Sending them does not mean that new leaders leave the ministry team. It simply means they are given specific ministry responsibility. Each new leader is still accountable to the ministry team and its leader.

As the ministry team matures, the members continue to meet to encourage one another in their personal lives and ministry. They no longer go out in twos as they focus on people in the community; rather, they take someone from their own Small Group in a With-Me effort to minister to others in the community.

When team members realize that their first priority is people, not program, then the leader can begin to allocate responsibilities for details of the program, according to each person's gift(s). One person may be gifted in the type of leadership responsibilities that are required of a Small Group coordinator, the person who receives the reports of the Small Group leaders. One person may be talented and gifted at leading singing. Some of them will most surely be ready to lead Small Groups of their own. Others who are gifted with evangelism could form evangelistic teams, and so on.

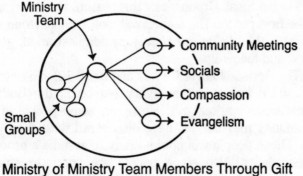

Ministry Team

Community Meetings

Socials

Compassion

Small Groups

Evangelism

Ministry of Ministry Team Members Through Gift
Challenging Program Responsibilities
Figure 3

This order of choosing leaders for an organization is different from the way most churches do it. Most of the time we look for a person who is capable and talented in certain areas and give them the responsibility for running the program. However, as you can see, we literally push them into making the program a priority so that people take a back seat. In focusing on the two areas of ministry—to the individual first, and to the group next—people in the Discipleship Community begin to minister the way Jesus and the Apostles taught us to serve. (See fig. 3) Every person on the ministry team has a personal ministry to people and an ability to take a part—even though it may be small—in the community program. Each member of the team can discuss people and program concerns and offer solutions.

A key person on the ministry team is the Small Group coordinator. This is someone who will work to help people form Small Groups and to help Small Groups find more people. The continued growth of the individual and the quality of the whole Discipleship Community is totally dependent on the participation of as many persons as pos-

sible in the Small Groups. For this reason, the coordinator
is the first person the leader will look for, someone who
will be faithful to do the necessary administration, phone
work, and follow-up.

The Apostle Paul (1 Cor. 12 and Rom. 12) and Peter (1
Pet. 4:10) indicated that every person in the Body of
Christ has a spiritual gift. However, some people in the
community may not yet have discovered what their gifts
are. These people will not be ready to assume a program
responsibility. Also some people are not interested in
becoming part of a program; others do not feel they have
the time. What do you do with these people? You encourage them to focus on people in Person-to-Person and
Small-Group ministry. This is just as important a role as
having a program responsibility.

At this stage of the developing ministry team, sharing
program responsibilities may be quite threatening to the
Discipleship Community leader. But the leader needs to
share some things he or she has been doing up to this
point—such as teaching, song leading, publicity, Small
Group coordinating—if the people on the team and in the
community are to grow. Unless people are given true
responsibility (Send-Them) they will ultimately stagnate in
their growth and/or leave in frustration. This statement
leads us into our final stage.

Stage 4: The ongoing development of the ministry team.
Throughout each stage of development, the leader has
worked very hard to help the ministry team members gain
and build on their double focus of ministry—to build the
people in Person-to-Person and Small Group ministry and
to serve the community with their gifts in some program
or service capacity. As the Discipleship Community
matures, the leader's approach to ministry must become

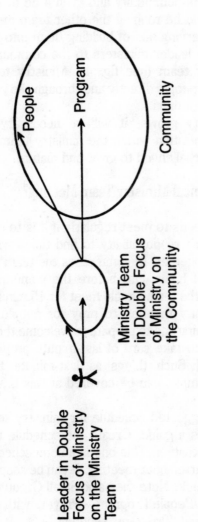

People

Program

Community

Ministry Team in Double Focus of Ministry on the Community

Leader in Double Focus of Ministry on the Ministry Team

Leader's Double Focus: Building persons on the Ministry Team and Enabling the Team's Double Focus on the People and Program of the Community.

Figure 4

ministry through people. The leader cannot possibly focus on every person in the community and even if he or she tried, the leader would be robbing the other team members of their joy of serving and of building them into the image of Christ. The leader ministers to the community through the ministry team (see fig. 4). Ministry team members minister to people directly and through the people in their own small groups.

As the community grows, it will be necessary to restructure the organization within the ministry team so the members will be challenged to grow and mature.

What Makes up a Typical Ministry Team Meeting?

The ministry team needs to meet regularly if it is to succeed. It is the leader's responsibility to find times when the team can all be together. In some cases the team can meet for a couple of hours just before the community meeting. In all cases the team should meet for 15 minutes before each community meeting to pray for people by name who will be coming and to prepare to welcome them. This is a good time to take care of last-minute program items—after prayer! Such things as last-minute task assignments, for example, can be covered at this time if appropriate.

Following is a suggested schedule for ministry team meetings. Use this as a guide. Create the schedule that works best in your situation. This one is a noon schedule for a one-and-one-quarter-hour meeting. It can be adapted for any time of the week. Note the basic Small Group format of Word—Share/People/Program—Prayer, with the addition of "People" and "Program" sections.

12:00	Gather	Eat lunch during meeting.
12:10	Word	Briefly share a passage of Scripture
12:25	Share	Team members briefly share personal needs and blessings.
12:40	People	Discuss people in your fellowship by name in order to plan ministry to them.
12:55	Program	Discuss key group building concerns. Work out details after ministry team meeting.
1:05	Prayer	Pray for personal needs in the ministry team, people in the community by name, and the group (program).
1:15	Dismiss	End on time.

The order may be changed if the team can share their lives better right before prayer—(Word—People/Program/Share—Prayer).

During the *Word* portion of the meeting, the leader will read a verse or two, explain the context of the verses and encourage team members to share what the verse means and how they can apply them to their lives. Since the time is short (10 or 15 minutes), this cannot be an exhaustive Bible study or a lecture; nor can everyone be given time to speak. It will, however, give the group a starting place, and God will use it to impart much content as you continue this practice week after week.

During the *Share* time, members briefly share highlights of their week and prayer requests. Generally, this time is limited because the team needs to discuss the needs of the community. However, occasionally a ministry team member will have a personal need so great that the whole time is used to support that person. This is okay, because the team is first of all a supportive fellowship. They can focus on ministry to the community at the next meeting.

The ministry team discusses the needs of people in the larger community during the *People* portion of the meeting. This discussion is not allowed to become a gossip/judgment time; rather its purpose is to find ways to minister to the people. It is a candid, confidential assessment of where the people are, followed by a discussion of who is to focus on whom, and how it is to be done. The concern is how to build people. The following people-building assessment questions can be used:

Who is new? Who has been absent? Who is hurting? Who has a need? Where are people in Christian discipleship (new life, new mind, new life-style)? How can we help certain people bond to the group so that they can experience unity, develop friendships, and find a place to serve in the group? Which team member will focus on which person?

The amount of time spent on discussing people will depend on the number of people who need help and the time available. Team members should be assigned to people who have specific needs. "I notice that Bob has been absent the last two community meetings. Who will phone him?" "Alice is new. Will you, Joyce, and you, Phyllis, sit with her during the meeting tonight and introduce her to others?"

The ministry team must seek to challenge those people in the community who want to minister and/or use their leadership abilities and spiritual gifts in specific ministries. This is best accomplished when team members personally yoke with these people in one-on-one, With-Me time. To check out how well team members are accomplishing this goal, periodically list those people whom they are building or ministering in partnership. Include all of the willing-to-minister/leadership people in the community.

I asked one ministry team of eight people to list all those people they were working with who were willing to minister/lead. Each person listed about four names; but when the lists were put together there were only ten different people listed. Some of them were building the same people and were missing several others in the community who should have been attended to. This can be avoided if these people are discussed during the team meeting.

It is important for the leader to assign ministry team members to follow up on people concerns. If someone says, "John Smith is new," then a team member should phone him; maybe it should be the person who brought up his name. Follow-through is essential if the People portion of the meeting goes from discussion to ministry.

During the *Program* portion of the meeting, the leader seeks input on how the Discipleship Community and Small-Group meetings are going. Many program concerns will come up in the ministry team meetings: The songs are too slow; they're too fast; there's too much talking and not enough focus on God; Bible study is boring; new people are not bonding with the group. Even though the concerns should be brought up during the Program part of the meeting, the details of solving them need to be taken care of outside the ministry team meeting by those responsible for the particular areas.

The time when the members start to pray should be set and held to; otherwise the program concerns will consume all remaining time and prayer becomes an afterthought.

As the community grows in number, the leadership team will find that program concerns will also grow. Ministry teams of large communities or of Congregations will become program management teams. One meeting each month will be spent discussing program and significant pastoral care issues. During this meeting, the team needs to review the two ministry assessment questions so that they can keep sight of their double focus of ministry—building the person and building the group in Bonding Factors and life-style. That way, the other team meetings can concentrate more on the Word—Share/People/Program—Prayer, with program concerns coming just before prayer. A ministry team must be led and trained to spend the majority of its time discussing people's needs and how to minister to them and build them in Christ more effectively.

During *Prayer*, every person on the team should be prayed for, whether or not they are present. Then the team prays for the people in the Discipleship Community. "Lord, please help us to find out why John has been absent from the group. Show us how we can build Jim and Jill in Christ. Restore Mary's health. Lord, help us find a Small Group for the Smiths." The team is a *ministry* team when it prays for people by name, and not only for such Program concerns as, "Please, Lord, help the meeting to go well. Bring us visitors. Speak through our teacher."

The ministry team should meet together for 15 minutes before the community meeting so that they can pray for people by name who will be attending the meeting; also it is a good time to take care of last-minute program details. Take care of the program concerns after you pray for the people. Often God leads you in ways to solve the program problems.

The ministry team becomes the heart of your ministry. They are the leader's "few," the people he or she will know most personally and will build most deeply in Christ. They will become friends of the heart, co-laborers with the leader in ministry; and they will also build the leader in Christ. "Iron sharpens iron, so one man sharpens another." (Prov. 27:17).

No ministry team is perfect. There will be disagreements and frustrations. Some people will seem to grow very slowly (as Philip did, John 14). Yet people on the team will learn to serve each other and serve the wider Discipleship Community. God will work in your life, in the team's life, and through them into the lives of many others.

CHAPTER 14

Building the Congregation

B uilding a Congregation that pulses with life is the dream and vision of every pastor and every enthusiastic member of a church. A church that is vibrant and alive is one that is concerned with the well-being and Christian maturity of every individual and with the Body as a whole: the double focus of ministry that works to build both the person and the group into the image of Jesus Christ.

If you feel that your church is lacking in life and focus, then it may be time to begin a people-building ministry within your Congregation. Revitalization of the Congregation begins with a statement of purpose, proceeds to needs assessment, and moves into goals and program. This is a necessary process, coupled with the grace of

God, if a Congregation is going to experience healthy growth and vital life.

After assessing your Congregation to determine where it now is and where you would like it to be, you need to decide where you must begin to build. This book includes four basic ministry patterns which you can adapt, depending on where your Congregation is. Those four patterns are: (1) Person-to-Person Ministry; (2) Small Groups; (3) Small Group Movement; (4) Discipleship Community.

Which one will you need to choose? How are you going to build your Congregation? Let us call attention to a couple of "Don'ts" first.

1. Don't drop or drastically alter an already existing program of the Congregation.

2. Don't issue abrupt changes in the ruling board's meeting format in order to make the meeting fit the Word/ Share/Prayer pattern.

3. Don't try to recruit everyone in a new program at the start.

These are the "don'ts"; now let us talk about some of the things you must do.

How to Begin

Individual renewal in a Congregation begins when the pastor and/or church leaders start to pray for renewal and spiritual growth. Since spiritual maturity is brought about only by the Holy Spirit, prayer is the place to start. A pastor or other leader to whom God is speaking will need to take the initiative. Along with the prayers, proclaim the message of what it means to have a new life in Christ and how Christians can grow in that life. Growth in discipleship must be a genuine congregational purpose and emphasis which can come about only by preaching, teaching, and modeling the Christian life-style.

After that, begin to work with those who indicate an interest in growth. You may do this in Person-to-Person ministry and by forming your first Small Group Movement or a Discipleship Community. Hopefully, those people in your Congregation who already have leadership positions will be among those who show interest in beginning something new that will lead toward stronger growth of the individual and of the group as a whole. But if the present leaders do not respond, take heart. In time, people who are maturing spiritually in the Small Groups will begin to surface in committees and on boards. Instead of trying to build leaders into growing Christians, growing Christians will develop into leaders.

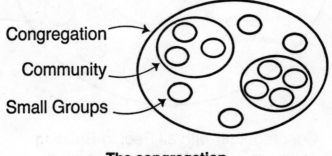

Congregation

Community

Small Groups

The congregation

Figure 1

One way to visualize the ministry pattern of Jesus Christ is to compare it with a series of concentric rings, like ripples in a pool into which you have thrown a pebble. Jesus ministered to the larger circle at the same time He focused on the few in the center. A vibrant Congregation is like a pond into which an increasing number of pebbles

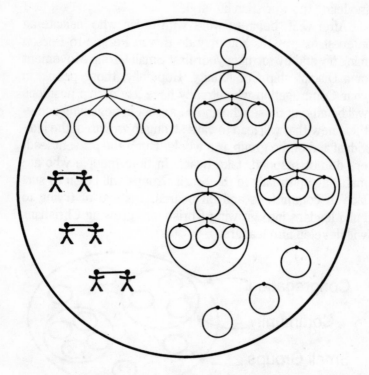

Congregation with all People-Building
patterns: Person to Person Ministry;
some independent Small Groups; an
organized Small Group Movement, and
several Discipleship Communities.

Figure 2

are thrown. Several groups of concentric ripples widen
out, overlap, and reinforce one another as people are
equipped to build one another and go out to serve others.
(See fig. 1.)

Choosing a People-Building Pattern

All four people-building patterns may be used to build people (see fig. 2). All have advantages and disadvantages
depending on particular situations in the church. All will
change the lives of the people and the life of the Congregation. You must assess your particular church to see which
pattern or patterns will be most effective. It depends on
the size and culture of your church, and the congregation's
receptivity to Small Groups and new ministry concepts.

The small church. Most churches in the United States
are small, numbering under 250 members. They are Discipleship Communities in which all the people know one
another or know about one another. Even though your
church may be small you can still use all of the people-
building patterns; however, as a pastor or leader in a small
church, you may have to do some creative thinking to find
ways to introduce new concepts and patterns.,

For example, the idea of a Small Group in a small
church might unsettle some people in the Congregation
who feel that they are one big family. A painless way to
start a Small Group is for a person or couple in the church
to begin to host a weekly open house Bible study in their
home, maybe after a Sunday or Wednesday night service.
Although many will respond at first, the novelty will wear
out for some and only those interested in this form of fellowship will continue to attend. The rest of the church will
see this group as open to all and not as a threat. In time,

the host will have a "small group" to lead in a pattern along the line of the Word/Share/Prayer triangle. If the group regularly exceeds 15 people, the pattern of building a Discipleship Community could be followed.

Existing ministries in the small church, such as a women's group or a couples' group, may be enhanced through the introduction of People-Building Principles and programs. If a new ministry is developed, the People-Building Principles can be built into the organization of the new ministry. The small church offers many opportunities for building individuals and the Body through the principles of Prayer, Care, With-Me, Word and Send-Them.

The larger church. Once a church begins to exceed 250 in membership, it moves into the category of middle-size or large church. Middle-size churches typically have 300 to 800 members with one or two full-time staff. Larger churches with 1,000 or more members have multiple staff and are very complex organizations. Large Congregations are characterized by multi-nested units with many Discipleship Communities and Small groups. As new communities form, the leaders and ministry teams of those communities must maintain commitment to the leadership authority structure of the Congregation. Such commitment is crucial to ensure that the communities within the church are not competitive but are supportive of one another. For example, if a person leaves community A and goes to community B, it is OK; he or she is still in the same Congregation.

Churches with multiple Discipleship Communities may have junior and senior high youth communities, a women's community, a community of both men and women, a singles community, a college/career community, and perhaps a senior citizen community. Each community may have

Small Groups within them. Additionally, however, there will be independent Small Groups within the Congregation that are not part of a Discipleship Community. Each community and Small Group participates fully in the activities of the whole Congregation, such as Sunday worship and other church-wide events. A multiple-community church is like a shopping mall, offering something for everyone. The leaders come from the professional staff and qualified members of the congregation, and the financial support from the church budget.

As the number of communities increases in a Congregation, some kind of coordination is necessary in order to help people find a "home" in the church, offer training and encouragement to community leaders, and see that scheduling of the many overlapping community activities does not overschedule people or conflict with the Congregation-wide activities. Responsibility for such coordination can be assigned to a staff member in cooperation with an elder, deacon, Christian education committee, or a special committee created for this purpose.

Some Practical Examples

Following are descriptions of different ministry situations. If you are the person on whom God has laid the burden of growing people in the image of Christ, which people-building pattern would you choose to begin with? Responses to each scenario follow the examples.

1. For eight years you have been a member of a small church in a community of 5,000 people. Approximately 75 people are actively involved in the church. You have a Sunday morning and Wednesday evening service. The pastor is very supportive of the Small Group concept. How would

you go about forming a people-building program?

Response: Since your whole Congregation numbers well under 250 people, yours is a Discipleship Community. You could initiate person-to-person ministry. With the pastor's support, you could begin a Small Group Movement by organizing two or three Small Groups to meet in homes, perhaps following the Wednesday evening worship service. If child care is a problem, or the hour would be too late to be practical, you could have each group choose their own meeting time.

2. You are associate pastor on a staff of three in a 900-member church that has a full program schedule. You are responsible for Christian education and the deacons. You have an excellent relationship with the senior pastor and the other staff member. What patterns for building people could you adapt?

Response: Since your church already has groups of all sizes and mixtures, you could begin any of the four people-building patterns. If you choose to begin a Small Group movement or a Discipleship Community, someone would need to devote a great deal of time to the organization and ongoing responsibilities, such as yourself or an elder or deacon. If your own schedule is too busy, you may be more effective if you begin to change an existing ministry by incorporating more of the principles of building people and groups.

3. You are part of a 400-member church that was founded in 1917. The pastor has been there three years. Although he is generally receptive to Small Groups, he is not personally involved in one, nor does he wish to work with them. He believes the church program is busy

enough without adding something else. You have a cordial relationship with him, but you have never worked together. What pattern would you select.

Response: Since your pastor is not very supportive of a Small-Group program, you would not be able to effectively launch a Small Group movement or a Discipleship Community. You could, however, focus on a few people yourself in a Person-to-Person ministry. Also, your pastor would probably have no objections to your starting a Small Group Bible study.

4. You are the senior pastor of a church of 1,600 members. There are six others on your staff. Your primary responsibilities are preaching, staff and ruling board leadership, and pastoral care. Worship is well attended and people are engaged in a variety of programs. Yet you feel that your church needs more vitality and a more intense program that will help the people to grow in the image of Christ. Which patterns do you think would be most effective in your situation?

Response: You could initiate any or all of the patterns for building people. So that the venture would be exciting and vibrant, and to model commitment to building people, you would begin to focus on a few yourself and encourage other staff members and primary leaders in your church to do the same. You may begin a Small Group that would practice the Prayer/Care/With-Me/Word/Send-Them master principles for building people.

You could also form a Discipleship Community. See the chapter on Forming the Discipleship Community for guidelines. It is not enough for a staff person, committee, or sub-group to be "in charge of discipleship or building people." Ultimately, the senior pastor, staff, and every leader must model it if all of the people in the Congregation are to be built.

5. You are the pastor of a 200-member church. In addition to Sunday morning services, your church has a women's group that meets Tuesday mornings and a youth group that meets Sunday evenings. What patterns could you select?

Response: Depending on how you approach them and how receptive the leaders are, the women's group and the youth group could each begin to add people-building elements such as weekly Small Group opportunities, and becoming more aware of the Bonding Factors. You probably could also begin a new ministry using any of the people building patterns such as a Person-to-Person ministry at lunch; a Small Group in the evening or at breakfast. You could begin a Discipleship Community on Wednesday evening using the ideas we spoke about in chapter 11. At the normal Wednesday night meeting, the community could meet together for teaching and worship, then divide into their Small Groups and either remain at the church for the Small Group time or (preferably) disperse to homes for Small Group meetings.

Assess, Plan, and Act

Three steps need to be taken before you actually begin whichever people building plan you choose.

First, you need to assess your ministry. Whether you are beginning a people building program in a church, a neighborhood, at work, or on a campus, you need to think about the make-up of your ministry so that you can choose the best pattern or patterns for your particular situation.

Think about the distinctive culture of your ministry-age, location, denominational affiliation, etc. All the factors that make your group unique. Every church has its own "feel," its own personality, history, stories, and standards of acceptable behavior. Then you can choose which of the four ministry patterns you believe can be adapted to your group according to its culture.

Next, assess your church's existing schedule of programs. This way you can see if you can use an existing program or if you will have to start a totally new one. If you begin a new one, you will have to see when your church can schedule it.

Last, assess your own schedule. When can you be committed to a discipleship effort? As you make these assessments, confer with the leaders of your church or ministry setting, seeking their support. And of course, pray for wisdom!

Plan your strategy. Review the checklists in the Appendix section of this book and modify them to fit your particular needs. Ask the person-centered and group-centered assessment questions and review the principles of ministry so that your program will meet needs through the double focus of ministry. Read the chapter on Implementing a Plan.

If you choose one of the many "commercial" programs available on the market for your people-centered program, you will need to adapt it to fit your particular situation. Pre-packaged programs can work well and serve a purpose in the church. Some of them use the principles of ministry very effectively, but they typically fall short when it comes to teaching the People-Building Principles that will move the individuals and the group toward growth.

Begin with the unique needs of your people and with

the Principles of Ministry. Then plan a people-building program by adapting one of the four building patterns in this book, or adapt a commercial program to best use the Principles of Ministry.

Act on your plans. Set a tentative beginning date during the *Assessment* step. Feel free to experiment and invite others to join the experiment. Set a three-month trial period, then re-assess. As you take the first step in a people-building ministry, God will lead you to the next step.

Building people can be frustrating. One-to-one ministry will lead one person into great growth, yet leave another one adrift in apathy. Just getting a Small Group going requires a great deal of effort. And a Discipleship Community program can take off with great enthusiasm and growth, or it can dwindle and drag.

Ministry is a practice. It is not a science that consistently predicts behavior or results. A great many other influences seek to shape the same people we seek to build. We need to apply the biblical principles the best we can to people of differing needs and levels of spiritual hunger. What we have described in this book will give you the best possible environment where people can grow. The results we leave to God.

Ministry is a life-style. Not only do we practice People-Building Principles in the planning a program (group life-style), we also practice them personally. Pray daily for each person, by name, whom you are growing in Christ. Care for them. Involve them in With-Me fellowship and ministry. Share the Word with them and Send-Them to ministries of their own.

CHAPTER 15

Getting Started

Whatever role you may have in your church, you can have a ministry that builds people. Since you are reading this book, I assume you already sense that God is sending you to serve the people who interact in your life and to grow in Christ along with them. To make your service for Christ more effective, you should choose one or more of the people-building patterns we have described and intentionally begin to practice the principles of ministry. As you build people in your own life you will be equipping them in turn for the work of the ministry.

Now that you have completed the preceding chapters, it is time to do some personal assessment and get your plans underway.

How is your personal growth in Jesus Christ? Are you growing in your relationship with Him? Are you growing in your knowledge of Scripture? Are you seeking to grow in your Christian life-style guided by the *Three Relationships*—with the Triune God, the Body of Christ, and the World, by practicing the *Spiritual Disciplines* of renewal, Word and prayer, family, fellowship, stewardship, ministry and work? You do not have to be fully matured yourself before you can begin to build others; but you need to be growing.

How well are you practicing the double focus—on the individual and on the group? Have you already determined which "few" you can begin to build? Do you know what your personal ministry is in the Body of Christ? The important thing is not that you already have a few or that you already have a place of service; rather, it is that you maintain consistent movement toward both. If you already have a "few," then choose one of the people-building patterns and get them together. If you know where you would like to use your gifts and energy in the group, begin to serve in that place.

How much time are you willing to give in this new venture? Perhaps your life is already filled with activities. What will you have to change or give up in order to begin this important ministry? One pastor, upon learning the steps to building people, said, "I'm too busy for discipling." His life revolved around program administration and preaching twice a week. Building people through Small Groups and Discipleship Communities takes time because they develop slowly. However, ultimate fruit will offer the greatest joy and promise for the future of your church.

Seek others in your fellowship who will join you in beginning a discipleship ministry. Look for a few who have a heart for God and a heart for people and who will share with you in the work of launching the people-building ministry, whether it is Person-to-Person, in a Small Group, a

Small Group Movement, or a Discipleship Community.

Be sensitive. Bringing change into an existing Community or Congregation requires sensitivity and care. The "Silly-Putty principle" is a good one to observe. If you attempt to stretch it quickly, it breaks. But if you pull it with consistent, gentle tension, it stretches smoothly. Some people and groups stretch and change easier than others. Be sensitive to ways to help your fellowship move into new patterns of life-style.

Be creative. All the patterns for discipleship ministry in this book are flexible. Adapt the ones that have the potential to best fit your unique ministry. The principles of person-building and group-building are universal and apply everywhere. The way you implement them will depend on the needs of *your* people.

Rejoice in differences. The people you build will all be in different levels of growth all the time. Some will be like the apostle Paul, hungry to grow in Christ. Others will be like Philip, who after three years with Jesus still did not grasp the relationship between God the Father and Jesus (see John 14:8-11). Some will be like Nathaniel, without guile and willing to grow. Be glad they are different from one another and from you. Tailor your ministry to meet their various needs.

Believe God. Building people is ultimately God's personal ministry. We labor with Him, using principles we learn from His Word and relying on the power of His Holy Spirit. Trust the Spirit to work with you to help people grow; expect growth to occur.

Joy comes as we grow in Christ, recognizing the peace

and the abundant life which He gives. Greater joy comes as we become instrumental in seeing other individuals and the whole Body grow in the image of Christ, alive and vibrant in response to the ministry we offer.

"Freely you received, freely give" (Matt. 10:8).

APPENDICES

Appendix A
CONTENT CHART

LIFE-STYLE RELATIONSHIPS OF THE BODY OF CHRIST	ESSENTIAL KNOWLEDGE	BASIC KNOWLEDGE	INTERMEDIATE KNOWLEDGE	ADVANCED KNOWLEDGE
Relationship with the Triune God: Father, Son, and Holy Spirit	The gospel of Jesus Christ: Promises of God Problem of sin Provision of Jesus Christ Decision of faith (PPPD)	The role of faith in the Christian life How to grow in faith The authority of the believer (spiritual conflict)	The attributes of God Gospel in depth: law and grace, the Old and New Covenants Redemption, regeneration, justification reconciliation sanctification glorification	Systematic theology, e.g., Christology and soteriology Christian creeds and confessions

Renewal	The Lordship of Jesus Christ The filling of the Holy Spirit Repentance Confession and forgiveness Holy Communion	Forgiving others Handling temptation Coping with trials and difficulties	The person and work of the Holy Spirit Pain and suffering
Word	How to develop a personal Bible study and prayer time Three Life-style Relationships Seven Spiritual Disciplines	Bible study methods Thinking theologically Bible verse memorization Knowing God's will Overview of the Scriptures How to teach the Bible	Hermeneutics (biblical interpretation) Homiletics (preaching) Ethics

Worship	How and why to worship with others How to worship alone	The sacraments: baptism and communion Means of worship: praise and thanksgiving, music, prayer, Scripture, sermon, sacraments	Theology of worship
Prayer	How to pray	Conversational prayer The prayer covenant Prayer partners Prayer in the Scriptures Kinds of prayer: meditative, urgent, silent, listening, fasting, journal writing	Theology of prayer

Relationship with the Body of Christ: The church	Importance of a church fellowship to a growing Christian	Biblical view of the people of God—origin, purpose, destiny Maturity of the Body of Christ	Ecclesiology (theology of the church) Church history Denominational perspectives
Family	The Christian family The single life	Christian parenting Communication: learning to dialogue Hospitality	Theology of relationships
Fellowship	The nature of the Body of Christ The small group	How to develop interpersonal relationships How to love the unlovable Conflict management How to find a church when you move	Theology of relationships

Stewardship	Biblical financial principles The life-style of generosity	Tithing, offerings, and alms Managing a personal budget Stewardship of all possessions Time management	Theology of stewardship
Ministry	Servanthood How to care How to build people in Christ Serving with your gifts	The double focus of ministry Principles of ministry Ministry to the grieving Counseling the confused and hurt Equipping ministry Healing ministry Spiritual gifts Leadership How to lead a small group	Theology of ministry (this book) Pastoral care

Relationship with the World	The ministry self-concept: I am sent to help and witness to the people in my life	How to lead a discipleship community / How to lead a congregation	Community vision: Help and witness in the community	World vision: help and witness in the world / Missiology (theology of missions)
Compassion	How to help other people	Counseling the confused and hurt / Diagnosing the ills in our culture / Becoming salt in society		Theology of compassion and justice

Evangelism	How to share the gospel	Life-style evangelism Apologetics: the defense of the Christian faith	Theology of evangelism
Work	Work as serving Jesus Christ Excellence in work	Ethics Ministry to fellow workers	Theology of vocation

Appendix B
The Small Group Sheet

Small Groups . . .

> DO offer friendship
> DO accept people just the way they are
> DO provide support in times of need
> DO encourage each person to walk with Christ
> DO NOT force anyone to speak if they wish to remain silent
> DO NOT require its members to be Bible scholars
> ARE a place where thinking adults can struggle together with the meaning of the Bible, can offer support to another, and seek God's best for life.

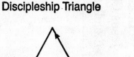

Discipleship Triangle

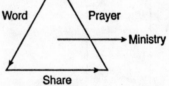

Word   Prayer

→ Ministry

Share

The following schedule can be adapted to fit the time your Small Group meets together:

> 45 minutes   Bible study or discussion of some study material. Share special insights which you received during your own study. The leader should see that everyone who wants to has a chance to speak.

45 minutes   Share blessings and needs. Where have you seen God at work in your own life through people, events and things?

15 minutes   Pray conversationally using the *S*'s of conversational prayer: Subject by subject; Short; Simple; Specific; Silent periods; Small Groups; Speak up.

Refreshments and time to chat a bit.
Disperse for ministry at home and at work

Suggestions:
Stick to the schedule so that you can end on time and still offer opportunity for people to talk to each other.

Sit around a table; you will find that discussion is intensified.

Be flexible. If someone in your group is experiencing a difficult, hurtful time, change your format and minister to him or her.

Hold refreshments until after the Word/Share/Prayer time; they should also be the kind that will not require the hostess to leave the group to prepare.

Review the Small Group Commitments every four to six months.

1. Priority. Every person will be at the meeting unless prevented by illness or other significant reason.
2. Punctuality. The group begins and ends on time.

3. Confidentiality. This is crucial. What a person says in confidence is shared in trust. Broken confidentiality is the fastest way to destroy unity, relationships and ministry.
4. Prayer. Pray regularly for the group and for each person in the group by name. Sometimes group members choose prayer partners who pray for each other daily and with each other weekly (often over the phone). Such partners may change every week or every month.
5. Personal prayer and Bible study. Every person will engage in regular Bible study and prayer between group meetings.
6. No giving of advice unless counsel is requested.
7. No arguments.
8. Confess your *own* needs (not those of other members).
9. Affirmation and vulnerability. When we are vulnerable and open ourselves to share deep inner thoughts, feelings, and experiences, we must be in an atmosphere of affirmation. A person who opens up and shares something personal and is then laughed at, ridiculed or criticized may never open up again.

Appendix C
Checklist for Starting a Small Group

Following is a sequence of events that many Small Groups go through. Some of these steps will be carried out by the person starting the group. Others will be agreed upon by the whole group. The more of these steps you can accomplish before the group begins the better.

Check when completed

1. _____ Gain the approval of your pastor or board.
2. _____ Decide whether the group will be open or closed:
   a. Open group—visitors and new members always welcome
   b. Closed group—membership by invitation only.
3. _____ Set your beginning date.
4. _____ Set your meeting time, both beginning and ending.
5. _____ Set the term of your Small Group. How many weeks will your Small Group commit to one another? Four months is a typical term, after which the people may continue to meet if they wish or can open up the group to new members.
6. _____ Decide which Small Group Commitments to propose to the group. These are outlined in Appendix B.
7. _____ Write out a schedule for your meeting times, using the Discipleship Triangle Word/Share format.

8. _____ Choose the material you will be studying—which book of the Bible or commercial study book.
9. _____ Invite seven to ten people using one of the following options:
   a. Private—extend invitation to individuals
   b. Public—extend invitation to entire fellowship.

Who are these people? Write down their names.

_____   _____

_____   _____

_____   _____

_____   _____

Appendix D
Checklist for Starting
Small Groups by Recruitment

1. _____ Gain the necessary approval of your pastor or board.

2. _____ Decide with your pastor or leader which committee, board, or leadership team will be responsible for the Small Group ministry.

3. _____ Recruit a Small Group coordinator or become that person yourself. The coordinator will coordinate and initiate the remaining steps.

4. _____ Set the starting date for the first Small Groups.

5. _____ Recruit and train potential Small Group leaders (see chapters 9 and 10).

6. _____ Recruit Small Group members by:
   a. A private invitation by each group leader
   b. A public invitation to the whole church or fellowship.

7. _____ Develop ongoing ways to recruit new people for Small Groups and to help Small Groups who need more people.

Appendix E
Checklist for Starting
Groups on a Renewal Weekend

1. _____ With pastor, board, and appropriate committees decide on a date and subject of the renewal weekend.

2. _____ Recruit a committee and leader to oversee the event. Responsibilities may include:

   a. Guest speaker arrangements
   b. Registration
   c. Small Group coordinator
   d. Facility and equipment arrangements
   e. Food and refreshments
   f. Publicity
   g. Books and materials
   h. Music
   i. Child care
   j. Other _____
   _____ .

3. _____ The person or a committee in charge of Small Group organization to do the remaining steps.

4. _____ Recruit people willing to lead Small Groups for six weeks following the event.

5. _____ Meet to train the leaders in the Word/Share/ Prayer format.

6. _____ Prepare sign-up sheets for people who want to register for a Small Group or who need more information.

7. _____ Coordinate with the guest speaker so that he/ she will highlight the Small Group opportunity during the weekend and will give time for people to sign up for Small Groups.

8. ____ After the weekend, assign people to group leaders after praying about who to place with whom.

9. ____ Ask Small Group leaders to be prepared to call the people who signed up and meet with them the first week after the renewal weekend.

10. ____ Follow up with the leaders after three weeks. Ask them to discuss the future of their group during its fifth meeting. Remind them to give opportunity for people to drop out of the Small Group after the six-week trial period without feeling guilty; at the same time, the leaders should encourage people to continue. Ideally, these same leaders will remain with their Small Groups. If not, ask for suggestions of who in the group might continue as leader.

Appendix F
Checklist for Starting
Small Groups by Division

1. ____ Gain necessary approval and support from the pastor, board and any committees involved.
2. ____ Pray the prayer of selection and begin to compile a list of potential Small Group members. Choose people who will eventually be able to lead their own groups.

_____   _____

_____   _____

_____   _____

_____   _____

3. ____ Decide when the group will meet.
4. ____ Set the dates for the term the first Small Group will meet, such as September through November.
5. ____ Plan the Small Group meeting format (see chap. 9).
6. ____ Invite eight to twelve people into the first Small Group. Explain to them the plan to divide in six months (or whatever time limit you set) and they will start new groups.
7. ____ Lead the group using the Word/Share/Prayer pattern until they understand it. Then rotate the lead so that each person or couple may practice the format.

8. ____ When the time approaches for the first Small
   Group to divide:
   a. ____ Review chapters 9 and 10 to more
   fully train the members to become
   leaders.
   b. ____ Ask the group members to prayerfully
   begin to develop lists of people to
   invite into the next generation of
   groups. The whole group could pray
   for these people.

9. ____ The first Small Group divides and each person
   or couple recruits the people they have prayed
   for. In six months (or whatever time limit you
   set) these second generation groups may divide
   again. Periodically, all the groups could gather
   for an evening of inspiration and fellowship. The
   Small Group coordinator meets regularly with
   the leaders to train and encourage them.

Appendix G
Checklist for Developing a Discipleship Community

1. _____ Gain necessary approval and support from the pastor, board and appropriate committees.

2. _____ Recruit a few who will serve with you as the preliminary ministry team (see chap. 13 as a guide). Meet weekly or regularly to plan and pray.

3. _____ Decide when the Discipleship Community will meet each week. Coordinate this with the church calendar.

4. _____ Set the dates for the first term, such as September through November.

5. _____ Plan the meeting format.

6. _____ Decide where the community will meet.

7. _____ Invite everyone to come. Do this by public announcements in the church, through bulletins, and by personal invitation.

8. _____ Begin the weekly community meetings with a focus on teaching and fellowship with the whole group as planned in step 5.

9. _____ Ask a member of the ministry team to be the Small Group coordinator, or fill that role yourself.

10. _____ The coordinator recruits and trains Small Group leaders from those attending the community meeting. Plan to start enough groups to accommodate everyone who is interested in Small Groups. Use chapters 9 and 10 to train leaders.

11. ____ Get those who are interested into Small Groups and get the groups going. This is a process that requires some attention as to who is put with whom so that the Small Group chemistry will be as good as possible. Part of the weekly ministry team meeting should be devoted to this process of getting the groups going as people indicate interest. Remember that Small Groups are to be offered as a desirable option but are not a requirement for attending community meetings. Small Groups are something that many people will not be ready for immediately, maybe never, but in time some will become interested.

12. ____ Look for people who may be qualified to become members of a ministry team (see chap. 13).

Appendix H
People-Building Lists

*Three Ingredients of
Ministry*
(chaps. 1, 2)

1. People
2. Principles
3. Practice (life-style,
   program)

*The Double Focus of
Ministry* (chap. 2)

1. The person
2. The group

*Three Life-Style
Relationships*
(chap. 3)

1. Triune God
2. Body of Christ
3. People in the world

Eleven Life-Style Marks
(chap. 3)

1. Renewal
2. Worship
3. Word
4. Prayer
5. Family
6. Fellowship

*Four Group Life-Style
Functions (WIFE)*
(chap. 7)

1. Worship
2. Instruction
3. Fellowship
4. Expression

Bonding Factors
(chap. 6, 7)

1. Unity
2. Relationships
3. Ministry

Discipleship Triangle
(chaps. 5, 9)

1. Word
2. Share
3. Prayer
4. Ministry

*Three-Step Planning
Process* (chap. 8)

1. Needs Assessment
2. Principles of Ministry
3. Program Planning

From *The Vibrant Church* by E. Stanley Ott. The pages in this Appendix section may be reproduced.

7. Stewardship
8. Ministry
9. Compassion
10. Evangelism
11. Work

Seven Spiritual Disciplines
(chap. 3)

1. Renewal
2. Word and prayer
3. Family strength
4. Fellowship with Christians
5. Stewardship of money
6. Ministry to others
7. Work

Five People-Building Principles
(chap. 4)

1. Prayer
2. Care
3. With-Me
4. Word
5. Send-Them

Two Assessment Questions

1. How can we build each person in the image of Christ?
2. How can we build our group in the image of Christ?

Four Ministry Patterns

1. Person-to-Person Ministry (chap. 5)
2. Small Groups (chaps. 9,10)
3. Small Group Movement (chap. 11)
4. Discipleship Community (chaps. 12,13)

Notes

Chapter 3
1. F.F. Bruce, *The Epistle to the Hebrews* (Grand Rapids: Wm. B. Eerdmans Publishing Co., 1964), p. 110, note 2.
2. Chuck Miller expresses the "three priorities" as (1) A progressive commitment to Jesus Christ; (2) a progressive commitment to the Body of Christ; (3) a progressive commitment to the work of Christ in the world. *Discipling Ministry Seminar* (El Toro, CA: Barnabas, Inc., 1977).
   Ray Ortlund says of these three priorities: (1) Wherever you are spiritually, commit your heart again to God; (2) Commit yourself to the Body of Christ; (3) Commit yourself to the world—your work in it, your witness to it. *Lord, Make My Life a Miracle* (Ventura, CA: Regal Books, 1974), pp. 2-3.

Chapter 6
1. I was introduced to the concept of the web of relationships by Chuck Miller, *Discipling Ministry Seminar.* Donald McGavran also speaks of this concept in *The Master's Plan for Making Disciples* (Pasadena: Church Growth Press, 1982).
2. C. Peter Wagner, *Your Church Can Grow* (Ventura, CA: Regal Books, 1976), p. 7.
3. James R. Tozer, *A Shared Adventure* (Lima, OH: C.S.S. Publishers, 1984).
4. Chuck Miller, *Discipling Ministry Seminar* (El Toro, CA: Barnabas, Inc., 1977), pp. 55-57.

Chapter 7
1. C. Peter Wagner, *Your Spiritual Gifts Can Help Your Church Grow* (Ventura, CA: Regal Books, 1979).

Chapter 9
1. Everlyn Christenson, *What Happens When Women Pray* (Wheaton, IL: Victor Books, 1975), pp. 38-51.
2. Elton Trueblood, *The Company of the Committed* (New York: Harper & Row Publishers, 1961), pp. 74-75. Used by permission.

Chapter 10
1. Charles M. Olsen discusses the small group life-cycle—initiating, enabling, terminating—in *Skills-Awake* (Atlanta: Lay Renewal Publications), n.d.

Chapter 12

1. James R. Tozer with Daniel W. Pawley, "Small Groups: How One Church Does It," *Leadership,* Vol. 4, No. 4, Fall 1980, pp. 58-66.

More Ministry Resources from Regal Books

Broken Members, Mended Body—Kathi Mills   More than a how-to-make-your-church-grow book; it is a book about broken people whose lives have been used by God to bring blessing to thousands. It is a story of vision, dreams and miracles.   5419585   ISBN: 0-8307-1302-6

Can the Pastor Do It Alone? A Model for Preparing Lay People for Lay Pastoring—Melvin Steinbron   Here is a proven program to equip lay people to help pastor the congregation.   5418925   ISBN: 0-8307-1171-6

How to Grow Your Church—Donald A. McGavran and Win Arn   This book applies proven principles of church growth from around the world to American churches.   5419394   ISBN: 0-8307-0238-5

Strategies for Church Growth—C. Peter Wagner   The latest strategies for fulfilling the Great Commission. Program ideas for pastors, mission boards, and evangelical coordinators.   5418914   ISBN: 0-8307-1170-8

Unleashing the Church—Frank Tillapaugh   Presents challenging ideas for extending a church's influence into the community. Learn how any church can shift its focus away from itself and reach out beyond its walls.   5418433   ISBN: 0-8307-1024-8

Up with Worship—Anne Ortlund   Practical ideas for expanding and revitalizing individual and corporate worship.   5417706   ISBN: 0-8307-0867-7

Look for these and other Regal books at your regular Christian bookstore.